The Big Fearon Book of
DINOSAURS

by Diane Calvert Burkle, Cynthia Polk Muller, and Linda J. Petuch
Scientific Consultant, Dr. Edward J. Petuch, Paleontologist

D1402616

Fearon Teacher Aids
Belmont, California

Designed and illustrated by Rose Schiafone Sheifer

Illustrations based on the work of Edward J. Petuch.

Entire contents copyright © 1989 by Fearon Teacher Aids,
500 Harbor Boulevard, Belmont, California 94002. However,
the individual purchaser may reproduce designated materials in
this book for classroom and individual use, but the purchase of
this book does not entitle reproduction of any part for an entire
school, district, or system. Such use is strictly prohibited.

ISBN 0-8224-0698-5

Printed in the United States of America
1. 9 8 7 6 5 4 3

CONTENTS

Why Study Dinosaurs?

Most children have a natural curiosity about "monsters." They feel both a fascination for and a fear of creatures which they consider to be monster-like. Dinosaurs are ideal subjects for children to pursue since they were, indeed, alive on Earth at one time. Dinosaurs fulfill most children's idea of what monsters should look like. Even with all we have learned about the dinosaurs, there are still many unanswered questions, leaving much room for children's imagination and further study.

▌ Teaching a subject interesting to children has endless possibilities for student involvement and mental growth. Since dinosaurs lived millions of year ago, their study is an excellent vehicle for other important concepts. "Digging for dinosaurs" or learning about how it is done teaches that the deeper you dig, the older the material unearthed. Students become aware of different strata of the earth's surface. Children learn the concept of time—that whole worlds have existed before human beings. The concept of extinction may also be taught; life is not static, but rather in a constant state of change. Adaptation to environment, food chains, and ecological niches are all biological concepts that may be explored using dinosaurs as motivating themes.

▌ Even though scientists disagree about what may have killed off the dinosaurs, they will all agree that it was, most probably, an ecological catastrophe of some kind. Extinction theories include the rise in the egg-eating mammals that killed off the unborn dinosaurs; a world-wide drought that caused starvation of the vegetarian dinosaurs and subsequently the meat-eaters; or the explosion of a nearby star that bombarded the Earth with high-intensity radiation, and killed most of the large animals. Recent evidence, however, strongly suggests that the main reason for extinction of dinosaurs was the impact of a giant asteroid which would have caused huge forest fires. This impact would have produced energies equal to 100,000 hydrogen bombs going off at once. The blast would have formed a gigantic dust and soot cloud that would have plunged the world into years of perpetual twilight. The loss of sunlight would have caused a worldwide cooling of climates and the destruction of much of the plant life. As in the drought theory of extinction, the dying of the plant life would have led to the starvation of vegetarian dinosaurs and their meat-eating predators.

▌ Supporting this last hypothesis are the recent discoveries of layers of meteoric dust and soot from burnt pine trees found in several places around the world. These layers correspond to the time of the extinction of the dinosaurs.

▌ Judging from the length of time of their existence, the dinosaurs were the most successful land animals that ever lived. Even very successful animals like these are susceptible, however, to massive changes in the environment. Using the demise of the dinosarus as an example, we are more aware of the fragility of the world ecosystem and the possibility of future disasters. When children study dinosaurs they understand the importance of protecting our environment.

How to
Use the Lessons
and Activities

This book has been organized into three sections:
1. The Mesozoic Era with its three main time periods (the Triassic, the Jurassic, and the Cretaceous),
2. The Plant-Eaters,
3. The Meat-Eaters.

For each of these sections, there are several dinosaurs to help teach important concepts.

▌ Triassic Period dinosaurs were small and primitive in form (not specialized). Some of them had feathers for warmth, and were the ancestors of later forms.

▌ Jurassic Period dinosaurs were more specialized in form (long necks, defensive spikes, bony crests). There were a greater number and variety of species during this period. Many of these dinosaurs were also much larger than earlier ones.

▌ Cretaceous Period dinosaurs were highly specialized (crests, horns, and very long necks and tails) and some were very large—reaching sizes of 24-30 meters (80-100 feet) in length.

▌ Plant-eaters developed useful features, such as long necks for reaching tall plants, and bony spikes as well as armor to prevent attacks. Some plant-eaters may have lived in herds for protection and developed camouflage patterns to help them hide from predators.

▌ Meat-eaters developed very sharp teeth, usually walked on two feet, and had very strong legs for running. Their teeth were very big in proportion to their mouths. They were generally smaller than the giant plant-eaters and their bodies were streamlined for faster movement.

Fact Sheets

Use the reproducible fact sheets on pages 29 through 35, 68, and 96 (Interesting Facts About Dinosaurs, Dinosaur Data at-a-Glance, The Mesozoic Era, The Triassic Period, The Jurassic Period, The Cretaceous Period, Plant-Eaters Poster, and Meat-Eaters Poster) for display, for booklets, and for planning your lessons.

Creative Writing Activities

Use the reproducible worksheet on **page 128**. This activity may be used successfully with any of the dinosaur projects in this book. You may want to write a story starter on the board to stimulate the children's imaginations.

Sample Story Starters:

The young Pachyrhinosaurus became separated from the rest of the herd. She realized her mistake and then. . .

"Peck. Peck. Peck." The baby Tsintaosaurus poked its head out of the shell, and for the first time, she saw . . .

The jungle was cool and quiet. As Minmi sat munching a leaf he saw. . .

Suddenly the wind shifted and Spinosaurus knew that. . .

The sun had just set and Stenonychosaurus awoke to see. . .

The earth was beginning to get warmer after a long cold winter. Kakuru, hungry and tired of searching for scarce food, saw. . .

Ask the students to draw a picture of the dinosaur in the box and to write a story about it.

At the prewriting level, record a student-dictated story on chart paper. Display the story. Let the children illustrate the story on their own papers. Children will enjoy taking turns dictating their stories.

Dino Scene Display

Purpose: To introduce students to the study of dinosaurs, and to create a handsome focus for dinosaur projects.

Materials: wall-sized piece of butcher paper approximately 2.5 x 2.5 m (8 x 8 ft). Strong tape, large sheets of colored construction paper, permanent black marking pens, crayons, paste, stapler, scissors

Procedure: Tape butcher paper to wall. Using the black marking pen, draw large landscape objects, such as palm trees, volcano, rocks, and water pool. See example above.

Allow small groups of students to take turns coloring the display. Let children, working in small groups, add three-dimensional fronds to the palm trees. Show the students how to fold 31 x 46 cm (12" x 18") sheets of green paper, lengthwise. Fringe the edges of the paper with scissors. Paste the fringed strips of paper to the trees. Pleat strips as necessary to fit on trees. Using available art supplies such as yarn, glitter, tissue paper, cotton , cellophane—ask students to create foliage such as ferns, grass, wet areas, and volcanic smoke. Use the Dino Scene Display as a background for students' drawings, creative writing, and as a focal point for dinosaur studies.

Dinosaur Days Display

Purpose: To introduce students to the study of dinosaurs and to create a focus for dinosaur units.

Materials: wall-sized piece of butcher paper 2.5 x 2.5 m (8 x 8 ft), opaque projector, dinosaur picture (from any of the worksheets) permanent black marking pen, crayons

Procedure: Tape the butcher paper to the wall. Project the dinosaur picture on the paper adjusting for the size needed. Trace the projected outline with the black marking pen. Remove the dinosaur outline from the wall, and place on the floor or other hard surface. Tape down the sheet of paper to prevent movement and ripping. Allow small groups of students to take turns coloring and adding designs to the dinosaur body. Encourage creativity. Rehang the dinosaur. Display additional dinosaur activities around it—worksheets, creative writing, and art projects.

Worksheet
Directions
and
Materials Lists

Triassic Period Dinosaurs

▌Syntarsus
Rice Feathers, page 39

Materials:
glue,
uncooked white rice,
crayons,
toothpicks,
1 worksheet per student.

Directions for students: Color the dinosaur completely. Using a toothpick, apply glue to a small feathered area of the dinosaur. Place rice grains onto the glue, continuing until the feathers are covered with rice.

▌Herrerasaurus
Tactile Skeleton, pages 41 and 42

Materials:
crayons,
toothpicks,
white glue,
scrap paper,
thinned tempera paints,
1 set of A and B worksheets per student.

Directions for students: Worksheet A— Trace the dinosaur's name and color the picture. Worksheet B—Place a small amount of white glue on a scrap of paper. Using toothpicks, carefully apply glue to the skull and bones of the dinosaur. Allow the glue to dry completely. When dry, touch the dinosaur bones. Variations: 1. Apply a thinned wash of paint over the entire worksheet. The glue on the bones should resist the paint. 2. Staple the body page on top of the skeleton page. Hold the pages up to the light to see an x-ray of the dinosaur's body.

▌Heterodontosaurus
Dinosaur Diet: Insects, pages 44 and 45

Materials:
scissors,
paste,
crayons,
1 set of A and B worksheets per student.

Directions for students: Color the dinosaur on Worksheet A and the objects on Worksheet B. Cut out the boxes which show what the dinosaur probably ate. Paste these boxes around the dinosaur.

▌Plateosaurus
Dinosaur Diet: Foliage, pages 47 and 48

Materials:
scissors,
paste,
crayons,
1 set of A and B worksheets per student.

Directions for students: Color the dinosaur on Worksheet A and the objects on Worksheet B. Cut out the boxes which show what the dinosaur probably ate. Paste these boxes around the dinosaur.

Jurassic Period Dinosaurs

■ Kentrosaurus
Toothpick Spikes, page 50

Materials:
crayons,
glue,
toothpicks,
1 worksheet per student.

Directions for students: Color the dinosaur. Using toothpicks and starting at the tip of the tail, apply glue to the spikes. Place a toothpick on each glued spike. Break the toothpick to fit if necessary. Continue until all the spikes are covered with toothpicks.

■ Dilophosaurus
Tactile Skeleton, page 52 and 53

Materials:
crayons,
toothpicks,
white glue,
scrap paper,
1 set of A and B worksheets per student.

Directions for students: Worksheet A— Trace the dinosaur's name and color the dinosaur picture. Worksheet B— Place a small amount of glue on a scrap of paper. Using toothpicks, carefully apply glue to the skull and bones of the dinosaur. Allow the glue to dry completely. When dry, touch the dinosaur bones. Variation: Staple the body page on top of the skeleton page. Hold the pages up to the light to see an x-ray of the dinosaur's body.

■ Coelophysis
Rice Feathers, page 55

Materials:
glue,
uncooked brown rice,
crayons,
toothpicks,
1 worksheet per student.

Directions for students: Color the dinosaur completely. Using toothpicks, apply glue to a small feathered area of the dinosaur. Place rice grains onto the glue, continuing until all the feathers are covered.

■ Camarasaurus
Design-a-Dino, page 57

Materials:
crayons,
thinned tempera paints,
paintbrushes,
1 worksheet per student.

Directions for students: With crayons, draw designs on the head, neck and back of the dinosaur's body (stripes, spots, mottled patches, zig-zags). Using thinned tempera paints, paint the dinosaur picture. The crayons should resist the paints.

Cretaceous Period Dinosaurs

■ Tyrannosaurus

Tactile Skeleton, pages 59 and 60

Materials:
crayons,
toothpicks,
white glue,
thinned tempera paints,
scrap paper,
1 set of A and B worksheets per student.

Directions for students: Worksheet A—
Trace the dinosaur body. Color the dinosaur. Worksheet B—Place a small amount
of glue on a scrap of paper. Using a
toothpick, carefully apply glue to the skull
and bones of the dinosaur. Allow the glue
to dry completely. When dry, touch the
dinosaur bones. Variations: 1. Apply a
thinned wash of paint over the entire
sheet. Glue on bones should resist paint.
2. Staple the body page on top of the
skeleton page. Hold the pages up to the
light to see an x-ray of the dinosaur's body.

■ Parasaurolophus

Giant Dinosaur, pages 62 and 63

Materials:
crayons,
scissors,
paste,
30.4 x 45.7 cm (12" x 18") sheet of
  manila paper per student,
1 set of A and B worksheets per student.

Directions for students: Color both
halves of the dinosaur. Cut them out.

Apply paste to the back of each dinosaur
piece. Place on the manila paper by
matching the two halves of the dinosaur.

■ Triceratops

Puzzle, page 65

Materials:
crayons,
scissors,
paste,
1 blank sheet of colored paper, and
1 worksheet per student.

Directions for students: Color the dinosaur. Separate the dinosaur picture by
cutting along all dotted lines. Reassemble
the puzzle by pasting the parts onto the
blank sheet of paper.

■ Ultrasaurus

Camouflage, page 67

Materials:
crayons,
1 worksheet per student.

Directions for students: Draw and color
designs on the dinosaur body (swirls,
spots, zig-zags, mottled coloring).

Plant-Eating Dinosaurs

MINMI

▌ Texture Painting, page 70

Materials:
crayons,
white glue,
1 worksheet per student.

Directions for students: Color Minmi. Using a toothpick, apply glue thickly to the spots on the dinosaur. Allow the glue to dry overnight.

▌ Stuffed Minmi, pages 71, 72, 73, and 74

Materials:
crayons,
scissors,
stapler/staples,
transparent tape,
2.54 cm (1") strips of newspaper,
1 set of A and B worksheets per student.

Directions for students: Cut out the dinosaur body sections on worksheet A (front and back). Match the two parts to make a Minmi, and tape the parts together on the back. Repeat with worksheet B (front and back). Color the dinosaurs. Match the two dinosaurs together (colored sides out) and staple them together. Leave an area on the back open so that strips of newspaper can be stuffed inside. After stuffing the dinosaur, staple the opening closed.

▌ Hidden Dinosaur, page 75

Materials:
crayons,
1 worksheet per student.

Directions for students: Find the Minmi hiding in the picture. Color the dinosaur and the rest of the picture. Discuss how animals' markings help to camouflage them for protection.

DACENTRURUS

▌ Toothpick Spikes, page 77

Materials:
crayons,
glue,
toothpicks,
1 worksheet per student.

Directions for students: Color the picture. Using a toothpick and starting at the neck, apply glue to a spike. Place a toothpick on the glued spike, breaking the toothpick to fit when necessary. Continue until all the spikes are covered with toothpicks.

■ Create-a-Scene, page 78

Materials:
crayons,
glue,
scissors,
green construction paper cut into pieces
  13 mm (1/2") wide by 5-8 cm (2-3") long,
1 worksheet per student.
(Optional: toothpicks to glue on dinosaur's spikes)

Directions for students: Color Dacentrurus, the water, trees, and grass. Fold the strips of construction paper in half lengthwise. Using scissors, fringe the sides of each strip. Spread glue on the central stem of a palm frond in the picture. Place the fringed construction-paper frond onto the "glued" frond. Continue until the palms are leafy and full. Optional: Glue toothpick spikes on the Dacentrurus. Add other greenery to the grassy areas.

■ Defensive Movement, page 79

Materials:
crayons,
scissors,
glue,
toothpicks,
metal brads,
1 worksheet per student.

Directions for students: Color the Dacentrurus and its tail. Color the Megalosaurus. Cut out the tail. Attach with a metal brad to the dinosaur's body. Using a toothpick and beginning at the neck, apply glue to a spike. Place a toothpick onto the glued spike, breaking the toothpick to fit when necessary. Continue until all the spikes are covered with toothpicks.

Allow to dry completely. The tail will move, showing how Dacentrurus and other dinosaurs used their spikes for defense.

TSINTAOSAURUS

■ Sequencing, page 81

Materials:
crayons,
1 worksheet per student.

Directions for students: Color the three pictures. Draw a line from the numeral 1 to the picture of what would happen first; draw another line from the numeral 2 to the picture of what would happen second; draw a line from numeral 3 to what would happen last in the series of pictures.

■ Puzzle, page 82

Materials:
crayons,
scissors,
paste,
construction paper,
1 worksheet per student.

Directions for students: Color the Tsintaosaurus and her nest of eggs. Separate the puzzle by cutting along the broken lines. Reassemble the puzzle by pasting the pieces on a blank sheet of paper.

■ Cut-and-Paste Crest, page 83

Materials:
crayons,
scissors,
paste,
1 worksheet per student.

Directions for students: Color the Tsintaosaurus' head. Color his crest. Cut out the crest. Match to the dinosaur's head and paste in place.

REBBACHISAURUS

■ Color-by-Number Crayon Resist, page 85

Materials:
crayons,
thinned purple tempera paint,
paint brushes,
1 worksheet per student.

Directions for students: Color the area with the numeral 1, yellow. Color the area with the numeral 2, brown. Color the area with the numeral 3, orange. Be sure to color heavily. Paint the entire worksheet purple.

■ Create-A-Scene, page 86

Materials:
crayons,
pencils,
glue,
green tissue paper, cut into 2.54 cm (1") squares,
2.54 cm (1") strips of brown construction paper,
1 worksheet per student.

Directions for students: Color the rebbachisaurus. Color the tree bark brown. Starting at the top of the tree, apply glue to a small section of the bark. Tear brown construction paper into small pieces and press onto the glue. Continue until the entire trunk has been covered with overlapping, torn paper. To add clusters of "pine needles" to the tree branches, apply a small amount of glue to the tip of a branch. Place a square of green tissue paper gently onto the eraser end of a pencil. Holding the tissue on the pencil, press the paper onto the glue; lift the pencil up. The tissue paper should "stand up" from the branch. Continue until the tree is covered with clusters of "needles."

■ Herbivore Dino-Diet, pages 87 and 88

Materials :
crayons,
scissors,
paste,
1 set of A and B worksheets per student.

Directions for students: Color the dinosaur and the Dino-Diet pictures. Cut out the squares with the Dino-Diet pictures in them. Paste the pictures that show the correct diet for herbivores around Rebbachisaurus.

PACHYRHINOSAURUS

▌ Design-a-Dino, page 90

Materials:
crayons,
watercolor paint,
paintbrushes,
1 worksheet per student.

Directions for students: Draw designs (mottled) with crayon on the back of the dinosaur. Using watercolor paint, paint the dinosaur.

▌ Dinosaur Match, page 91

Materials:
crayons,
scissors,
paste,
1 worksheet per student.

Directions for students: Match the fronts and backs of the dinosaurs. Color the back and front of each dinosaur part to match. Cut out the back parts. Paste them to the correct fronts.

CLAOSAURUS

▌ Measuring, page 93

Materials:
crayons,
small metal paper clips,
pencils,
1 worksheet per student.

Directions for students: Color the dinosaur. Beginning at Claosaurus' head and using the paper clip, measure the length of Claosaurus' body. Convert the number of paper clips to standard measure (refer to the scale). Write Claosaurus' length in the blanks.

▌ Matching Babies to Adults, page 94

Materials:
crayons,
pencils,
1 worksheet per worksheet.

Directions for students: Color the dinosaurs. Match the baby dinosaurs to the correct adult dinosaurs by drawing a line between the matching pairs.

▌ Matching Parts, page 95

Materials:
crayons,
pencils,
1 worksheet per student.

Directions for students: Color the pictures. Match the body parts to the correct dinosaurs by drawing a line from each picture on the left to the dinosaur on the right.

Meat-Eating Dinosaurs

KAKURU

▌Texture painting, page 98

Materials:
crayons,
white glue,
toothpicks,
1 worksheet per student.

Directions for students: Color Kakuru. Using a toothpick, dab glue thickly on the feathers. Allow the glue to dry overnight.

▌Measuring, page 99

Materials:
crayons,
small metal paper clips,
pencils,
1 worksheet per student.

Directions for students: Color the dinosaur. Beginning at Kakuru's head, use a paper clip to measure the length of Kakuru's body. Convert the number of paper clips to standard measure (refer to the scale). Write Kakuru's length in the blanks.

▌Snow Scene Block Puzzle, page 100

Materials:
crayons,
scissors,
paste,
blank paper,
1 worksheet per student.

Directions for students: Color the puzzle parts. Separate the worksheet by cutting on the solid lines. Assemble the puzzle by pasting the puzzle parts on a blank sheet of paper.

STENONYCHOSAURUS

▌Torn Paper Mosaic, page 102

Materials:
black crayons,
scraps of colored construction paper,
paste,
1 worksheet per student.

Directions for students: Outline the dinosaur's head with black crayon. Tear bits of colored paper into small pieces. Apply paste to a small area of the dinosaur. Place the torn paper onto the dinosaur so that the edges overlap. Cover the entire head with the torn paper.

▌Stenonychosaurus Diet, page 103

Materials:
crayons,
paste,
scissors,
1 worksheet per student.

Directions for students: Color the pictures. Cut out the six pictures below the dinosaur. Paste them around the dinosaur to show the correct diet.

▌ Night Scene Line Puzzle, page 104

Materials:
crayons,
scissors,
paste,
blank paper,
1 worksheet per student.

Directions for students: Color the night scene. Separate the puzzle by cutting along the solid lines. Reassemble the puzzle by pasting the pieces on a blank sheet of paper.

SPINOSAURUS

▌ Stuffed Giant, pages 106, 107, 108, and 109

Materials:
crayons,
scissors,
transparent tape,
stapler/staples,
2.54 cm (1") strips of newspaper,
1 set of A and B worksheets per student.

Directions for students: Cut out the two dinosaur body sections (worksheet A, front and back). Match the two parts to make a Spinosaurus, and tape the parts together on the back. Do the same procedure for worksheet B (front and back). Color the dinosaurs. Match the two dinosaurs together (colored sides out) and staple them together. Leave an area on the spine open so that strips of newspaper can be stuffed inside. After stuffing the dinosaur, staple the opening closed.

▌ Toothpick Spikes, page 110

Materials:
crayons,
glue,
toothpicks,
1 worksheet per student.

Directions for students: Color the Spinosaurus. Using a toothpick, place lines of glue on the spine of the dinosaur's back. Place toothpicks on the spine. Some toothpicks may need to be broken to fit the size of the spine.

▌ Design-a-Dino, page 111

Materials:
crayons,
watercolor paint,
paint brushes,
1 worksheet per student.

Directions for students: With crayons, draw designs on the head, neck and back of the dinosaur's body (stripes, spots, mottled patches, zig-zags). Using watercolor paint, paint the dinosaur.

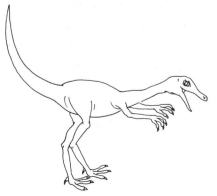

CERATOSAURUS

▮ Hinged Jaw, page 113

Materials:
crayons,
scissors,
paste,
metal brads,
1 worksheet per student.

Directions for students: Color Ceratosaurus. Cut out the head. Separate the head by cutting on the broken line. Cut out the teeth and paste them behind the jaws (6 uppers, 6 lowers). Attach the jaws together at the "dots" with a brad (place upper jaw over top of bottom jaw).

▮ Glittering Ceratosaurus, page 114

Materials:
crayons,
glue,
toothpicks,
large box lid,
glitter/shaker,
1 worksheet per student.

Directionsfor students: Color the dinosaur. Using a toothpick, apply glue thickly to horn, eye, claws, and the mottled areas of Ceratosaurus' body. Hold the worksheet over a large box lid and shake glitter over the glued areas. Allow the glue to dry before touching the glittering Ceratosaurus.

▮ Stuffed Tooth, page 115

Materials:
scissors,
stapler/staples,
2.54 cm (1") strips of newspaper,
1 worksheet per student.

Directions for students: Cut out both dinosaur teeth. Match both parts together, printed side out. Staple the edges together, leaving the wide part of the tooth open. Stuff with newspaper. Staple the open end of the tooth closed.

ALLOSAURUS

▮ Skeleton Rubbing, pages 117 and 118

Materials:
crayons,
toothpicks,
white glue,
blank paper,
1 set of A and B worksheets per student.

Directions for students: Worksheet A—Trace the dinosaur body. Color the dinosaur. Worksheet B—Place a small amount of glue on a scrap of paper for each student. Using a toothpick, carefully apply glue to the skull and bones of the dinosaur. Allow the glue to dry completely. Place a blank sheet of paper over the tactile skeleton and rub a crayon over the skeleton. Optional: Staple the body page on top of the skeleton page. Hold the pages up to the light to see an x-ray of the dinosaur's body.

▌Bag Puppet, pages 119, 120, 121

Materials:
crayons,
scissors,
medium-sized paper bag,
paste,
1 set of worksheets per student.

Directions for students: Color all three parts of the dinosaur. Cut out all dinosaur parts. Paste the tail on the front of the bag, near the opening. Paste the body, covering the base of the tail, on the front of the bag. Make sure the top of the body is under the flap of the bag. Paste the head on the top of the bag flap.

▌Hunting Scene Puzzle, page 122

Materials:
crayons,
scissors,
paste,
blank paper,
1 worksheet per student.

Directions for students: Separate the puzzle by cutting on the solid lines. Assemble the puzzle by pasting the puzzle pieces on a blank sheet of paper. Color the puzzle.

COMPSOGNATHUS

▌Crayon Resist, page 124

Materials:
crayons,
thinned blue tempera paint,
paintbrushes,
1 worksheet per student.

Directions for students: Color Compsognathus. Paint the entire worksheet with blue tempera paint.

▌Carnivore Dino-Diet, pages 125,126

Materials:
crayons,
scissors,
paste,
1 set of A and B worksheets per student.

Directions for students: Color the dinosaur on Worksheet A and the pictures on Worksheet B. Cut out the pictures. Paste pictures appropriate for a carnivorous animal on and around Compsognathus.

▌Matching Parts, page 127

Materials:
crayons,
pencils,
1 worksheet per student.

Directions for students: Color the pictures. Match the body parts to the correct dinosaurs by drawing a line from the pictures on the left to the dinosaurs on the right.

Glossary and Pronunciation Guide

Albertosaurus
(al-bert-o-sawr-us) "Lizard from Alberta" A meat-eating dinosaur that lived during the Cretaceous period.

Allosaurus
(al-o-sawr-us) "Different Lizard" A large, meat-eating dinosaur that walked on hind legs and had short front arms with three-clawed hands. It lived during the late Jurassic Period.

ancestor
A predecessor that is genetically related to the most recent living organism.

animal
Any member of one of the five kingdoms of living things (Animalia, Plantae, Fungi, Monera, Protista) that is characterized by having to eat in order to live.

Ankylosaurs
(an-kile-o-sawrs) "Fused Lizards" A group of plant-eating, armoured dinosaurs of the Cretaceous Period.

Apatosaurus
(a-pat-o-sawr-us) "Deceptive Lizard" A large, long-necked, plant-eating dinosaur (sauropod); more commonly known as Brontosaurus. It lived during the Jurassic Period.

Archeopteryx
(ark-e-op-tear-ix) "Ancient Wing" A feathered, birdlike animal which had small, sharp teeth. It lived during the late Jurassic Period and is believed to be the first bird.

asteroid
A large extra-terrestrial body, intermediate in size between a planet and a moon, which occasionally collides with larger celestial objects.

beak
Sharp-edged, flattened bladelike extension of the skull surrounding the mouth opening.

bipedal
Refers to animals that most often walk on their two back legs.

bird
A group of egg-laying animals characterized by being covered with feathers and derived from the same branch of dinosaurs as the Tyrannosaurus.

bone
Internal calcified structures used for support or protection.

Brachiosaurus
(brack-e-o-sawr-us) "Arm Lizard" One of the large, long-necked, plant-eating dinosaurs (sauropods) which lived during the Cretaceous

period. The name was derived from the fact that the front legs were longer than the back legs. Brachiosaurus had large nostrils at the top of its head.

Brontosaurus
(brawn-toe-sawr-us) "Thunder Lizard" A large, long-necked, plant-eating dinosaur (sauropod) which lived during the Jurassic Period. It is scientifically correct to call it Apatosaurus or "Deceptive Lizard".

Camarasaurus
(kam-air-a-sawr-us) "Chambered Lizard" A giant, long-necked vegetarian dinosaur that reached lengths of over 18.2 meters (60 feet) with a neck of more than 6 meters (20 feet). It lived during the Cretaceous period. Its name refers to the huge, hollow chambers of its skull. Remains are found in late Jurassic fossil beds in Colorado.

camouflage
Protective coloration pattern used to hide an animal from predators.

canine
Refers to the four elongated, pointed front teeth resembling those of dogs; the teeth are used for ripping and tearing flesh.

carnivorous
Refers to an animal that lives by eating the flesh of animals; meat-eating.

Ceratopsians
(sayr-a-tops-e-ans) "Horned Lizards" Plant-eating, horned dinosaurs which lived during the late Cretaceous; all are characterized by having a "frilled" neck.

Ceratosaurus
(sai-rat-o-sawr-us) "Horned Lizard" A meat-eating dinosaur that walked on its two back legs. It is the only known meat-eater to have a horn.

Claosaurus
(clow-sawr-us) "Branched Lizard" An early and more primitive, noncrested duck-billed dinosaur

(hadrosaur) which lived during the late Cretaceous Period.

Coelophysis
(see-low-fy-sis) "Hollow Form" A feathered dinosaur from the Jurassic fossil beds of New Mexico and Connecticut; had a bird-like appearance with long jaws filled with tiny, sharp teeth. Its name refers to its hollow, birdlike bones.

Compsognathus
(komp-sow-nay-thus) "Elegant Jaw" One of the smallest known dinosaurs. This meat-eater lived during the Late Jurassic Period.

crest
Flattened, platelike extension of the skull.

Cretaceous Period
(kree-tay-shous) This time period lasted from 135 million years ago to 65 million years ago. It is named for the chalk cliffs of southern England. During this period, the greatest number of types of dinosaurs appeared and the first grasses, grasslands and savannahs appeared.
   The last large dinosaurs died out at the end of the Cretaceous period. One dinosaur group, the birds, survived the asteroid event.

Dacentrurus
(dah-cen-true-roos) "Pointed Tail" A small, plant-eating dinosaur which lived during the late Jurassic Period. It had paired spikes running along its neck, back, and tail.

develop
Changing through time either in size or in the development of new features.

Dilophosaurus
(die-low-foe-sawr-us) "Two Crested Lizard" A 6-meter (20-foot) long carnivorous dinosaur from Arizona's Jurassic fossil beds. It had a characteristic double crest on its head.

dinosaur
An extinct prehistoric animal, probably related to birds. Scientists now think that dinosaurs were warm-blooded animals. Dinosaurs lived

during the Mesozoic Era. The earliest fossils are from the Triassic Period, the last from the late Cretaceous Period.

dorsal
Pertaining to the back of an animal (dorsal fin on a fish).

dust cloud
Large aggregate of microscopic particles of pulverized rock.

ecologies (ecology)
The relationships between organisms (plants and animals) and the environment. The study of these relationships.

extinct
Having died out; no longer existing after a certain time.

frill
A fanlike, bony extension to the back of the skull.

genus
A group of organisms that share distinctly defined similarities. There can be many species (kinds) of these organisms in the same genus. (Genus: Tyrannosaurid; Species: Tyrannosaurus rex, Daspletosaurus torosus, Albertosaurus libratus, Tarbosaurus bataar.)

Hadrosaurs
(had-row-sawrs) Group of plant-eating, duck-billed dinosaurs that lived from the middle to the late Cretaceous Period.

herbivorus
Refers to an animal that lives solely by eating vegetables and fruits; vegetarian; plant-eating.

Herrerasaurus
(hair-rare-a-sawr-us) "Dr. Herrera's Lizard" A Triassic Period carnivorous dinosaur from Argentina; 1.2-1.5 meters (4-5 feet) tall. It was named for Dr. Herrera, the discoverer.

Heterodontosaurus
(het-tear-o-dont-o-sawr-us) "Different Toothed Lizard" A .6-meter (2-foot) long Triassic period dinosaur from South Africa. It had sharp, canine teeth like a dog's, and it fed on large insects.

horn
An elongated, conical bony appendage usually attached to the skull of the dinosaur.

Ichthyosaurs
(ick-thee-o-sawrs) "Fish Lizards" Swimming reptiles of the Mesozoic Era with streamlined, fish-shaped bodies, highly specialized for swimming.

Iguanodontids
(e-gwan-o-don-tidz) "Iguana Teeth" A group of medium to large, plant-eating dinosaurs that usually walked on their back legs and used their tails for counterbalance, but were able to walk on all four legs as well. They lived from the late Jurassic Period to the end of the Cretaceous Period.

insect
A group of animals characterized by having a hard external skeleton and six legs.

Jurassic Period
(jur-ass-ic) The time period lasted from 180 million to 135 million years ago. It was named for the Jura Mountains of northwestern Switzerland. During this period, the first large dinosaurs and the first birds appeared.

Kakuru
(ka-koo-roo) "Rainbow Lizard" A small, meat-eating dinosaur which lived in a cold climate and was probably feathered for warmth. It lived during the early Cretaceous Period.

Kentrosaurus
(kent-row-sawr-us) "Pointed Lizard" A 5.5 - meter (16-foot) long vegetarian dinosaur from Tanzania, Africa Jurassic fossil beds; related to American Stegosaurus and had rows of spikes and plates along its back.

lizard
One of the kinds of reptiles characterized by being cold-blooded and scaly; usually having four legs.

Mesozoic Era
This time period lasted from 250 million years ago to 65 million years ago. It is known as the "Age of Dinosaurs" and is broken into three time periods: the Triassic, the Jurassic, and the Cretaceous.

Minmi
(min-me) A small, armoured, plant-eating dinosaur that lived during the early Cretaceous. It was named for a place in Australia.

Nemegtosaurus
(ne-met-toe-sawr-us) "Nemegt Lizard" A long-necked, plant-eating dinosaur (sauropod) which lived during the late Cretaceous Period.

Pachycephalosaurs
(pack-e-sef-a-lo-sawrs) "Thick-Headed Lizards" A group of plant-eating dinosaurs having very thick skulls which were probably used for defense and mating displays. They ranged in size from 1 meter (3 feet) to 8 meters (26 feet). They lived during the Cretaceous period.

Pachyrhinosaurus
(pack-e-rhino-sawr-us) "Thick-Nosed Reptile" An unusual looking horned dinosaur (an example of ceratopsians) that not only had short spikes around its neck frill but also had a coarse knob covering the snout, between its eyes. It was a plant-eater that lived during the late Cretaceous Period.

Parasaurolophus
(pair-a-sawr-o-low-fuss) "Like Crested Lizard" A 9-meter (30-foot) long vegetarian dinosaur from Cretaceous fossil beds of the southwestern United States and western Canada; had a long, crestlike tube attached to the back of the head.

plantigrade
Walking on the sole of the foot with the heel touching the ground, as bears and humans do; a plantigrade animal.

plate
A flattened, dish-shaped, bony, sharp-edged appendage usually attached to the neck and back of the dinosaur.

Plateosaurs
(plate-e-o-sawr-us) "Flattened Lizard" A 6-meter (20-foot) long vegetarian dinosaur from the Triassic fossil beds of Europe and South America; ancestor of Jurassic and Cretaceous long-necked dinosaurs.

Plesiosaurs
(please-e-o-sawrs) Marine reptiles of the Mesozioc Era that swam by using large flippers. These animals are not classified as dinosaurs.

predation
Living by preying on other animals.

protection
Any mechanism, either physical or behavioral, that deters attack or predation.

Pteranodon
(tear-an-o-don) "Winged and Toothless" One of the most advanced pterosaurs (flying reptiles). This animal appeared in the late Cretaceous Period and was an ocean-going fish eater.

Pterodactylus
(tear-o-dack-till-us) "Winged Finger" One species or kind of animal in the group know as pterosaurs.

pterosaurs
(tear-o-sawrs) "Winged Lizards" A large group of flying reptiles of the Mesozioc Era.

quadripedal
Refers to animals that usually walk on all four legs.

Rebbachisaurus
(re-back-i-sawr-us) "Rebbachi Lizard" A long-

necked, plant-eating dinosaur (sauropod) that had a "fin" down its back. It lived during the late Cretaceous Period.

sauropods
(sawr-o-pods) "Lizard Feet" A group of very large dinosaurs (some were the largest land animals ever) that had four feet with five toes each, elephantlike legs, long necks, and small heads. These giant dinosaurs lived from the late Triassic Period until the Cretaceous Period.

skeleton
A collection of articulated bones that supports the organism.

snakes
A group of limbless reptiles (cold-blooded and scaly).

specialize
In biology, to change or adapt organs, parts, or behavior to meet special needs; for example, having especially longs necks, having armor plating for defense, or eating only insects.

species
A population of living things that have similar physical appearances and that can or do inter-breed to produce living offspring.

spike
An elongated, conical, bony, hornlike appendage usually attached to the back or tail of the dino-saur.

Spinosaurus
(spine-oh-sawr-us) "Spiny Reptile" A large meat-eating dinosaur with a "sail" made of skin along its back. It lived during the early Creta-ceous Period.

Stegosaurus
(steg-o-sawr-us) "Roofed Lizard" A four-footed, plant-eating dinosaur having "fanlike" plates along its back and tail, and four sharp spikes at the end of its tail. It lived during the late Jurrasic Period.

Stenonychosaurus
(sten-o-nike-o-swar-us) "Narrow-Clawed Rep-tile" A lightly built, meat-eating dinosaur which had large eyes that enabled it to see and hunt for food at night. It lived during the late Cretaceous Period.

Styracosaurus
(sty-rack-o-sawr-us) "Spiked Reptile" A species or kind of ceratopsian (horned dinosaur) having long horns all along its neck frill. It lived during the Cretaceous Period.

Syntarsus
(sin-tar-sus) "Together Tarsal Bones" The name refers to the connected bones of the foot that are similar to the feet of birds. A 1.2-meter (4-foot) tall, feathered carnivorous dinosaur found in Triassic fossil beds of Zimbabwe, Africa. It had a crest on the back of its skull.

tibia
The lower bone of the leg (shin bone).

Triassic Period
(try-ass-ic) This time period lasted from 250 million years to 180 million years ago. It is named for three rock beds in southern Germany. During this period, the first dinosaurs appeared mostly small in size, and the first palm tree forests appeared.

Triceratops
(try-sayr-a-tops) "Three horned Face" The name refers to the horns on the face shield. A 9-meter (30-foot) long, 12 ton, rhinolike, vegetarian dinosaur from Cretaceous fossil beds of the western United States and Canada. It had one large horn above each eye and a smaller horn on its nose; a large, parrotlike beak; and the back of its skull was developed into a large, fanlike frill which protected its neck from attacks by carnivo-rous dinosaurs. Triceratops traveled together in large herds.

Tsintaosaurus
(sin-tao-sawr-us) "Reptile from Tsintao" A duck-billed dinosaur (hadrosaur) which had a solid

crest above its eyes, and lived during the late Cretaceous Period.

Tyrannosaurus
(tie-ran-o-sawr-us) "Tyrant Lizard" Giant Cretaceous carnivore reaching 12-meter (40-foot) lengths and standing over 6 meters (20 feet) tall. It is found in fossil beds in the southwestern United States and western Canada. It had giant cat-like claws on its hind legs and 15-centimeter (6-inch) teeth.

Ultrasaurus
(ul-tra-sawr-us) "Greatest Lizard" A 60-meter (200-foot) long vegetarian dinosaur from the Cretaceous fossil beds of Colorado. It had a , 24-meter (80-foot) long neck much like a giant giraffe. It was the longest, if not the largest, land animal that ever lived.

vertebrae
The bones forming the spinal column.

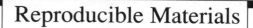

Posters, Activities, and Worksheets

INTERESTING FACTS ABOUT DINOSAURS

(based on the latest paleontological discoveries)

■ Dinosaurs were not reptiles, but were a separate group of animals.

■ Many dinosaurs, if not all, were warm-blooded like mammals and birds.

■ Some dinosaurs laid eggs, but it is now thought that many gave live-birth.

■ Some dinosaurs, particularly the smaller carnivorous species, were completely covered with feathers.

■ Many prehistoric animals that have previously been called "dinosaurs," such as the flying pterosaurs (Pterodactylus and Pteranodon), the porpoiselike ichthyosaurs, and the long-necked marine plesiosaurs, were not really dinosaurs at all, but were types of extinct reptiles.

■ Unlike reptiles, most dinosaurs were sociable animals, often traveling in large herds or family groups.

■ Unlike most reptiles, dinosaurs cared for their young. Some babies may have stayed with the mother for several years.

■ Many carnivorous dinosaurs hunted together in packs, much as wolves do today.

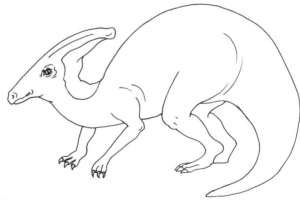

■ Not all dinosaurs lived in tropical areas. Many species lived in cold areas of Canada, Mongolia, and Argentina.

■ The last groups of large dinosaurs to become extinct were the giant, horned ceratopsians (Triceratops) and the hadrosaurs (Parasaurolophus). Based on recent fossil discoveries in Alaska, scientists think these last dinosaurs may have actually lived into the "age of mammals" (the Cenozoic era that we now live in).

DINOSAUR DATA AT-A-GLANCE

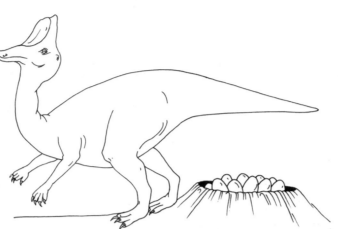

Family Life

Some dinosaurs laid eggs and hatched their young, while others may have given birth to live offspring. Recent evidence suggests that dinosaurs were more family oriented than previously thought. A family unit of mother and babies has been found in the the fossil beds of Montana. This may mean that mothers cared for and taught their young past the hatching stage. Some dinosaur mothers fed their babies predigested food. Remains of dinosaur nests show that the nests were elaborate, lined with leaves and twigs. The nests were elevated to keep out water. Some were very large, almost 4.6 meters (15 feet) in diameter. Dinosaurs used their claws to dig nests in the sand or mud.

Herding

Generally the large herbivores (plant-eaters) migrated in herds to follow food supplies. Staying together in large herds gave the animals some protection from predators. The babies of the animals that lived in herds may have been active immediately after birth and able to move with the herd, just as young calves and colts in modern-day herds are. Some herds may have numbered in the millions, much like buffalo herds on the great plains. Migrating dinosaurs may have travelled several hundred miles per year (Triassic dinosaurs in the Connecticut River Valley, United States).

Life Span

Although there is presently no scientific evidence documenting the average life-span of dinosaurs, some indirect evidence, such as growth rings on teeth and calcification of bones, suggests that some species may have lived about fifty years. Giant species may have lived to be over two hundred years old.

Color

Varied skin coloration (drab or bright) with stripes, spots, and/or patches served to camouflage and protect the animals.

Intelligence

Dinosaur intelligence appears to have varied according to life-style. As a general rule, carnivores were probably more intelligent than herbivores.

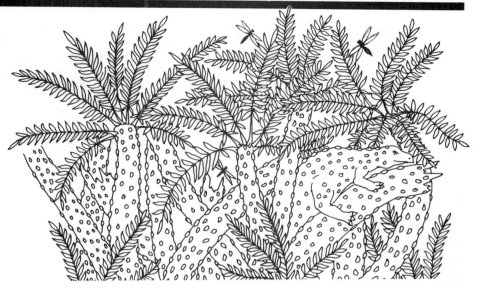

The meat-eating, hunting life-style demands greater intelligence for participation in social interactions (hunting in packs, social hierarchy, learned behaviors, refined hunting skills, and cooperation). Generally, the larger the brain size in proportion to the body, the greater the intelligence.

Teeth

Dinosaur teeth, unlike those of mammals, were shed and replaced by new teeth when broken, worn, or lost. Generally, tooth size indicates body size: the bigger the teeth, the bigger the body.

Tooth shape and size varied according to life-style. Carnivores had long pointed teeth, sometimes with serrated edges, for ripping and tearing flesh. Some dinosaurs had canine teeth that were used for grabbing prey. Herbivores had nipping and grinding teeth like those of horses and cows. These teeth were used for cropping and pulverizing plant matter.

Speed

The physical characteristics of the dinosaurs, such as body shape and strong hind legs, determined how fast or how slowly the animals moved. Dinosaurs with stocky bodies and thick legs probably were slower moving, possibly 9.3 km/h (15 m.p.h.). Dinosaurs that walked upright, with strong hind legs and considerable shorter forelegs, most likely moved at greater speeds, possibly 31 km/h (50 m.p.h.).

THE
MESOZOIC ERA

The Age of Dinosaurs

The Mesozoic era, which ranges from 250 million to 65 million years ago, is broken into three time periods: The Triassic (named for three rock beds in Southern Germany), the Jurassic (named for Jura Mountains in Northwestern Switzerland), and the Cretaceous (named for the chalk cliffs of Southeastern England). True dinosaurs, although small, first appear in the Triassic period. Throughout most of the Mesozoic era, the earth's climate was probably warmer and more tropical than it is today, although cooler climates began to appear during the Cretaceous period.

Besides dinosaurs, the first flowering, modern-looking plants appeared in the Mesozoic era. These first flowers were similiar to magnolias. During the Triassic Period, palm trees began to flourish. The first true grasses appeared in the Cretaceous period. The appearance of these modern-looking plants allowed the dinosaurs to develop many large vegetarian species. These plant-eaters, in turn, were the prey for large meat-eaters. So, in many ways, the development of the dinosaurs–from primitive, small types in the Triassic period to giant, advanced forms in the Cretaceous period–is directly related to the development of the Mesozoic plants.

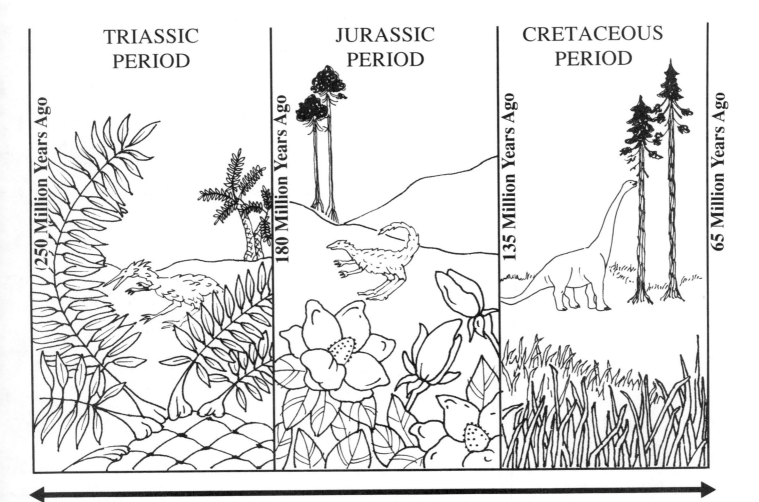

TRIASSIC PERIOD
JURASSIC PERIOD
CRETACEOUS PERIOD

(250 Million Years Ago)
180 Million Years Ago
135 Million Years Ago
65 Million Years Ago

Triassic Period

250 - 180 million years ago

The Triassic Period was the first of the three periods in the "Age of Dinosaurs." At the beginning of the Triassic Period, most species of dinosaurs were still primitive in form and small in size averaging almost 1 meter (3 feet) in height. At the end of the Triassic Period, many types had become quite large, like Plateosaurus, and were the ancestors of the more familiar, larger dinosaurs of the late Mesozoic era. Many of the small dinosaurs of the Triassic period were covered with feathers, probably for warmth. One group of these feathered dinosaurs later gave rise to birds.

Some Triassic Period Dinosaurs

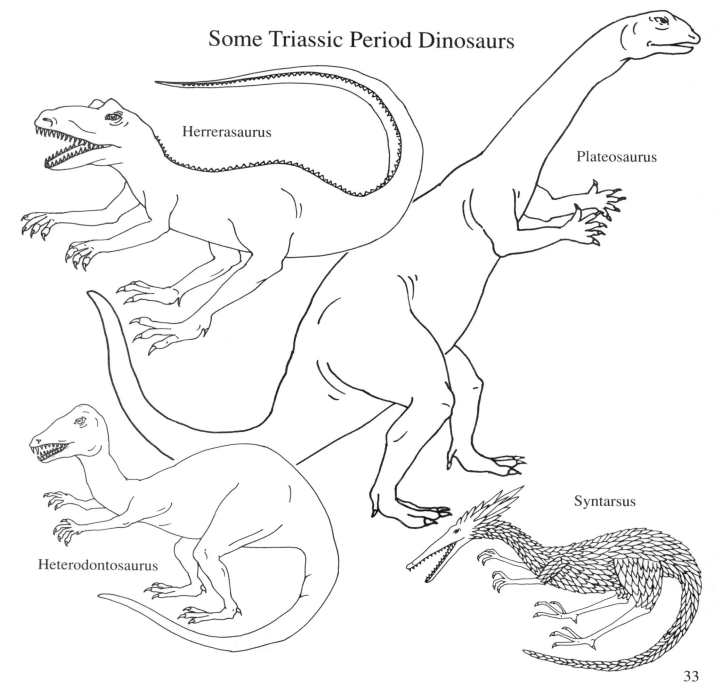

Herrerasaurus

Plateosaurus

Heterodontosaurus

Syntarsus

33

Jurassic Period

180-135 million years ago

During the Jurassic Period, the few, primitive species of dinosaurs of the Triassic Period gave rise to an explosion of hundreds of new types. The Jurassic period was really the first period of the Mesozoic era in which dinosaurs really began to rule the earth. During this time, the first giant species appeared, most noteworthy being the huge, long-necked sauropod dinosaurs, typified by Apatosaurus (Brontosaurus), Camarasaurus, and Brachiosaurus. Also during the Jurassic period, one group of small, feathered dinosaurs, related to the Triassic Period Syntarsus, developed long feathers on their forearms and tail and used these for gliding as they ran and jumped along the ground. A more advanced form of this group, Archeopteryx from the upper Jurassic period, is generally considered to be the first bird. By the end of the Jurassic period, many kinds of true, modern-appearing birds had arisen from Archeopteryx-type dinosaurs.

Some Jurassic Period Dinosaurs

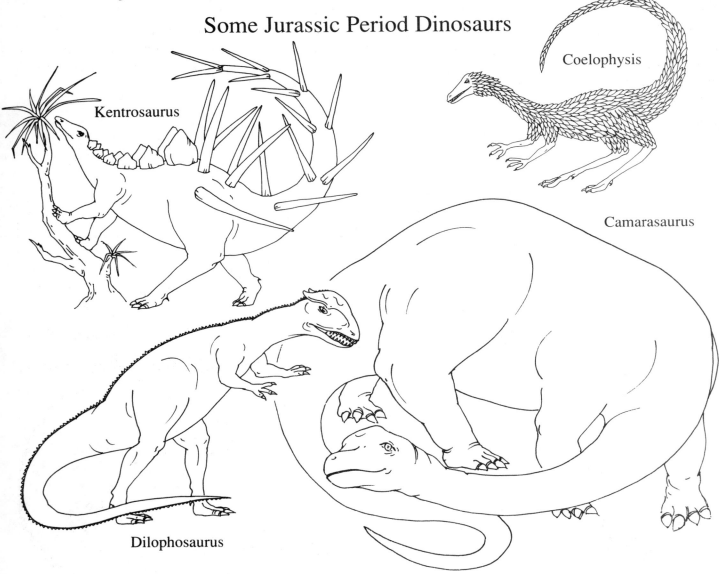

Kentrosaurus

Coelophysis

Camarasaurus

Dilophosaurus

Cretaceous Period

135 - 65 million years ago

One interesting pattern commonly seen in lineages of fossil animals is described in "Cope's Rule." This rule states that as animals develop through time, they generally become larger and larger. Most often, when creatures first appear, they are usually small and unspecialized. As time goes on, the small primitive form develops into larger and more specialized forms, until finally, the last and oldest species of a group are gigantic in size. "Cope's Rule" is especially obvious in the Cretaceous Period. The tiny dinosaurs of the Triassic Period, which developed into medium-sized dinosaurs in the Jurassic Period, became huge, monstrous types in the Cretaceous Period. Typical were such colossal creatures as Ultrasaurus, Tyrannosaurus, Albertosaurus, and Nemegtosaurus (similiar to Camarasaurus). At no time in the Earth's history has "Cope's Rule" been more obvious than at the end of the Cretaceous Period.

All of these fantastic animals disappeared almost abruptly about 65 million years ago. Scientists are still trying to discover the reason why they all died out so quickly. Recently, some new evidence has suggested that the earth was hit by a huge asteroid at the end of the Cretaceous Period. The resulting dust cloud would have produced a perpetual twilight, killing off many types of plants and plunging the world into a huge Ice Age. Many of the plant-eating giant dinosaurs may have starved to death, and the giant meat-eaters would have also died of starvation when their vegetarian prey disappeared. Only the small, feathered, warm-blooded dinosaurs that we call "birds" survived.

Some Cretaceous Period Dinosaurs

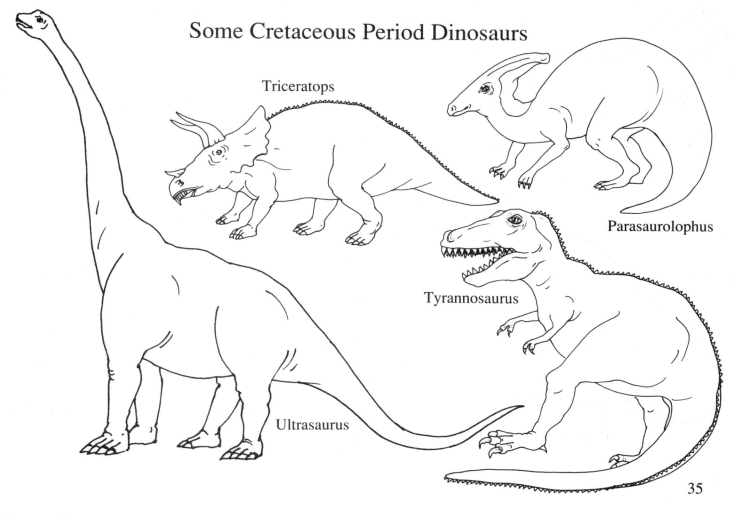

Triceratops

Parasaurolophus

Tyrannosaurus

Ultrasaurus

35

MESOZOIC ERA TIME LINE

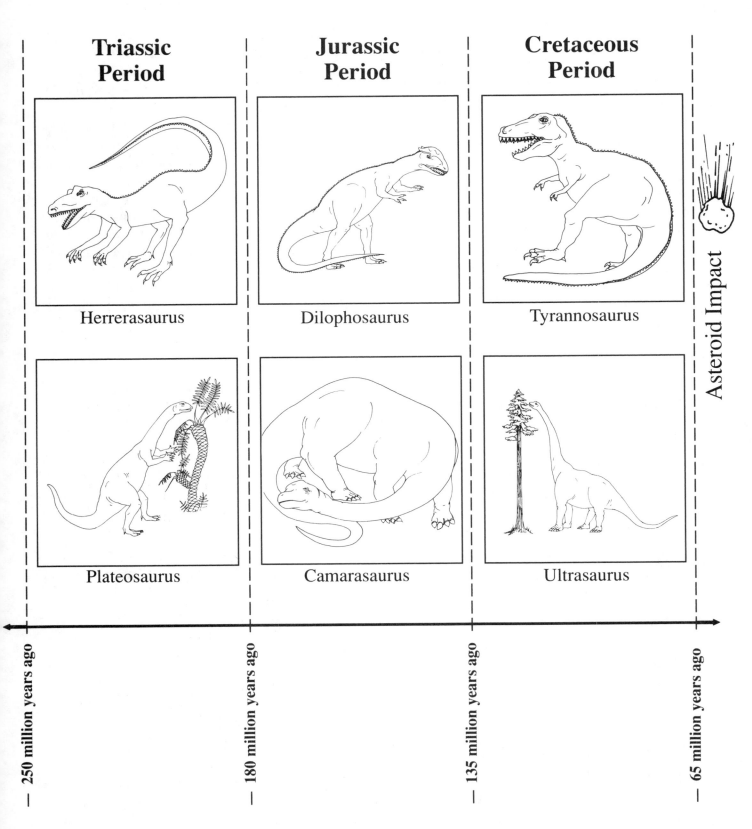

Triassic Period

Herrerasaurus

Plateosaurus

Jurassic Period

Dilophosaurus

Camarasaurus

Cretaceous Period

Tyrannosaurus

Ultrasaurus

Asteroid Impact

250 million years ago

180 million years ago

135 million years ago

65 million years ago

LAYERS OF THE EARTH
WITH FOSSIL REMAINS

YOUNGER

OLDER

Cretaceous Period

Ultrasaurus
70 million years ago

...first grasslands appeared; largest dinosaurs existed

Jurassic Period

Camarasaurus
150 million years ago

...first birds appeared; first true flowering plants appeared; medium-sized dinosaurs existed

Triassic Period

Plateosaurus
200 million years ago

...first palm tree forests appeared; first dinosaurs appeared, mostly small in size

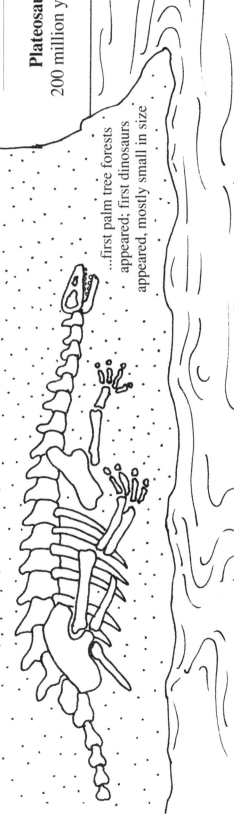

37

Syntarsus

Syntarsus (sin-tar-sus) "Together Tarsal Bones,"
Early Triassic Period

Originally found in Zimbabwe, Africa, Syntarsus weighed about
27 kilograms (60 pounds) and stood about 1.22 meters (4 feet) tall.
Like many of the smaller true dinosaurs, Syntarsus was probably
feathered. Unlike similar small dinosaurs, this African dinosaur
had a distinctive crest at the back of the skull. Syntarsus probably
fed on small animals such as lizards and snakes.

The Big Fearon Book of Dinosaurs © 1989

Syntarsus

Herrerasaurus

Herrerasaurus (hair-rare-a-sawr-us) "Mr. Herrera's Lizard,"
Triassic Period

Herrerasaurus was discovered in Argentina, and was first named
in 1963. This small animal, only about 1.2 - 1.5 meters (4-5 feet)
tall, was one of the early carnivorous dinosaurs. It probably fed
on other small dinosaurs.

Worksheet A

The Big Fearon Book of Dinosaurs © 1989

Worksheet B

Herrerasaurus Skeleton

The Big Fearon Book of Dinosaurs © 1989

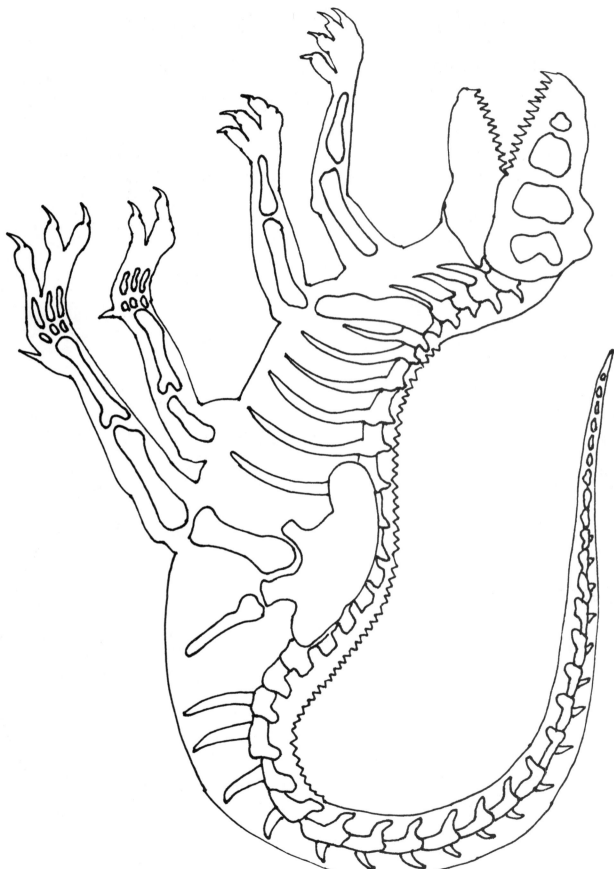

Heterodontosaurus

Heterodontosaurus (het-tear-o-dont-o-sawr-us)
"Different Toothed Lizard,"
Triassic Period

Heterodontosaurus was a native of South Africa, and was unusual among early dinosaurs because it had sharp canine teeth like a dog. A small dinosaur, only about .6 meter (2 feet) long, Heterodontosaurus probably fed on large insects such as cockroaches and dragonflies and small animals such as spiders.

Worksheet A

Heterodontosaurus Diet

The Big Fearon Book of Dinosaurs © 1989

Plateosaurus

Plateosaurus (plate-e-o-sawr-us) "Flattened Lizard,"
Triassic Period

Plateosaurus was one of the giants of the Triassic period, reaching lengths of over 6 meters (20 feet). It could stand and walk on its hind legs but appears to have preferred to walk on all fours. Plateosaurus had a long neck for reaching up into trees for tender succulent young leaves, and was probably the ancestor of the long-necked sauropod dinosaurs of the Jurassic and Cretaceous Periods (Apatosaurus, Diplodocus, Brachiosaurus). Plateosaurus has been found in Germany, France, and Argentina.

Plateosaurus Diet

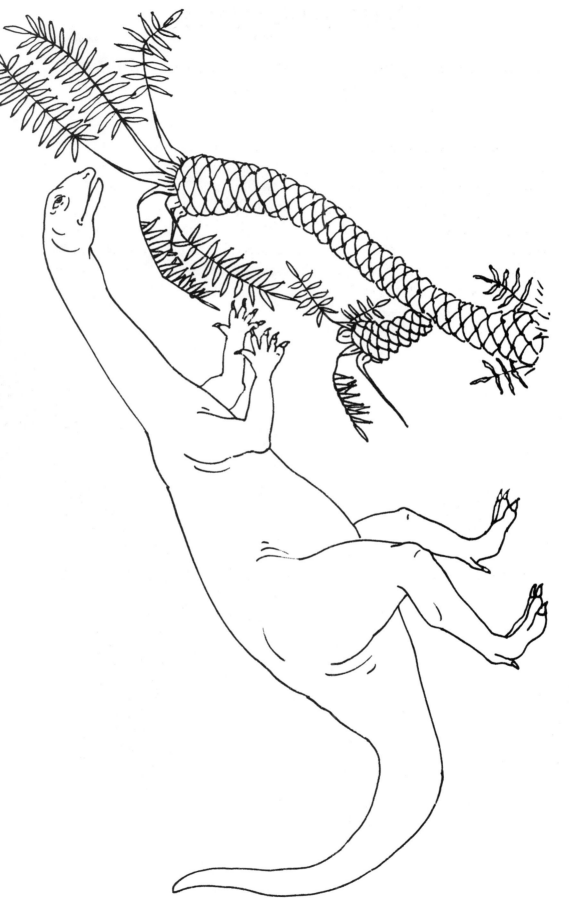

Name _____

Date _____

Plateosaurus   Diet

The Big Fearon Book of Dinosaurs © 1989

Kentrosaurus

Kentrosaurus (kent-row-sawr-us) "Prickly Lizard," Jurassic Period

Kentrosaurus was a close relative of the American Stegosaurus, but differed in having large spikes on the back half of the body and small plates on the front half. The spikes and plates were undoubtedly protection against attacks by large meat-eating dinosaurs. Kentrosaurus lived in Tanzania, Africa, grew to lengths of over 5 meters (16 feet), and was a peaceful plant eater.

Kentrosaurus

Dilophosaurus

Dilophosaurus (die-low-foe-sawr-us) "Two-Crested Lizard,"
Jurassic Period

Dilophosaurus is related to other meat-eating dinosaurs such as Allosaurus and the Cretaceous Period Tyrannosaurus. Dilophosaurus was the only one of its group to have two large bony crests on its head. The function of this double crest is still not known. This unusual dinosaur lived in Arizona, was about 6 meters (20 feet) long, and probably fed on smaller dinosaurs and lizards.

Worksheet B

Dilophosaurus Skeleton

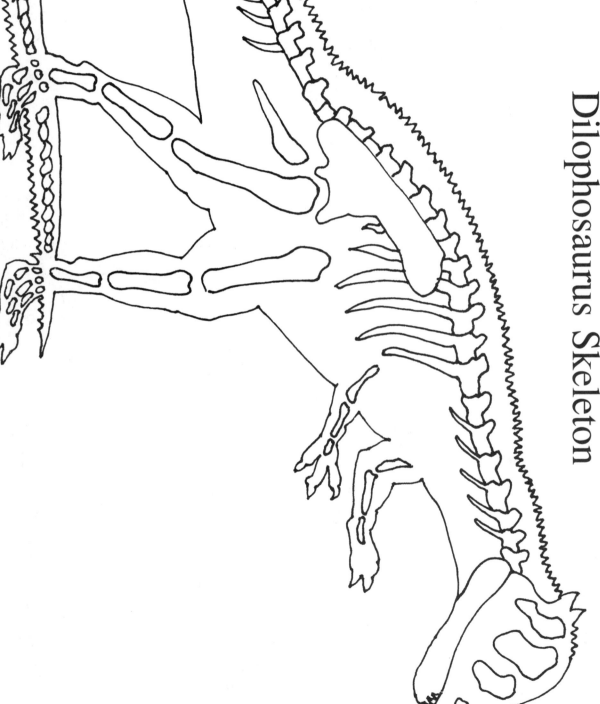

The Big Fearon Book of Dinosaurs © 1989

Dilophosaurus

Date

Name

Coelophysis

Coelophysis (see-low-fy-sis) "Hollow Cavity,"
Jurassic Period

Like the Triassic Period Syntarsus and other small dinosaurs, Coelophysis was probably covered with feathers. The feathers kept Coelophysis warm and were not used for flying. Although related to birds and birdlike dinosaurs, Coelophysis was the largest of this group of feathered dinosaurs, growing to lengths of 3 meters (10 feet). It had long jaws filled with tiny, sharp teeth, and probably fed on large insects and small animals such as lizards. Coelophysis bones have been found in New Mexico and Connecticut.

Coelophysis

Name _____

Date _____

Camarasaurus

Camarasaurus (kam-air-a-sawr-us) "Chambered Lizard,"
Jurassic Period

Camarasaurus was one of the largest of the long-necked dinosaurs that are called "sauropods." It was first thought that these giants had to float in water to support their oversized bodies and that they spent most of their time in lakes and ponds feeding on water plants. New discoveries and computer reconstructions of their skeletons, however, show that they were definitely land animals, and despite their huge size, had legs that were strong enough to support their great weight. They used their long necks to reach up into trees where they fed on leaves, just like giraffes. Camarasaurus grew to about 19 meters (60 feet) in length and had a 6-meter (20-foot) neck. It has been found in Colorado.

Camarasaurus

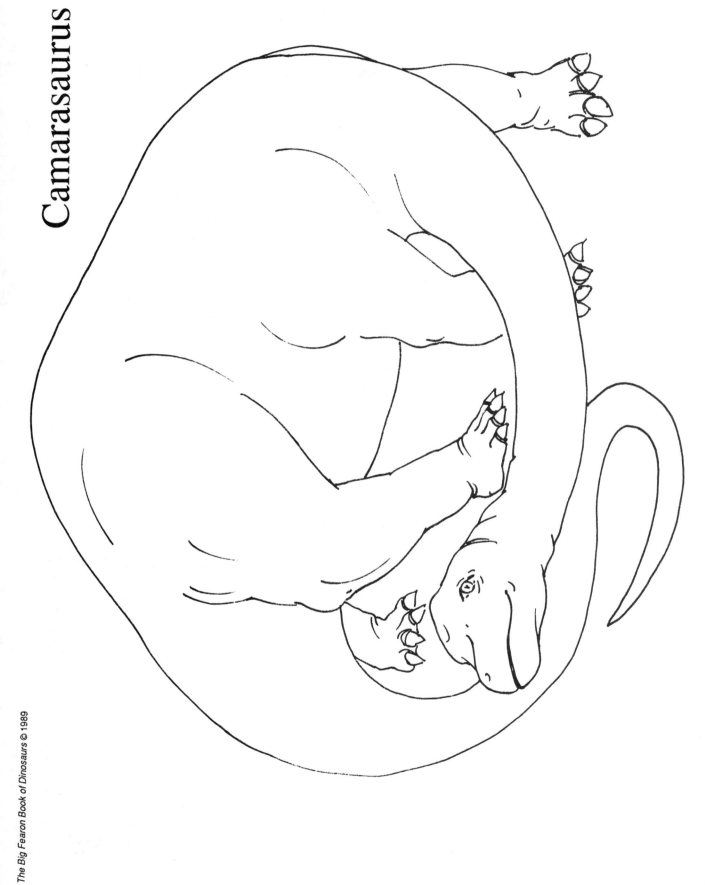

Name _____

Date _____

Tyrannosaurus

Tyrannosaurus (tie-ran-o-sawr-us) "Tyrant Lizard,"
Cretaceous Period

Tyrannosaurus is one of the best known dinosaurs and is a good example of the giant meat-eaters of the Cretaceous period. Although reaching over 12 meters (40 feet) in length and standing about 6 meters (20 feet) tall, Tyrannosaurus was not the largest of the meat-eaters. Bones of even bigger, and yet unnamed, species have been found in Mongolia, Canada, and England. Still, Tyrannosaurus was certainly a powerful hunter, having hind legs armed with giant, catlike claws, and having a huge mouth filled with 15-centimeter (6-inch) teeth. Recent studies suggest that Tyrannosaurus was faster moving and more slender than was once thought. This "tyrant lizard" lived in the southwestern United States and western Canada, where it hunted large plant-eating dinosaurs like Triceratops.

58

The Big Fearon Book of Dinosaurs © 1989

Worksheet A

Tyrannosaurus

Name _____

Date _____

Name _____ Date _____ 60

The Big Fearon Book of Dinosaurs © 1989

Worksheet B

Tyrannosaurus Skeleton

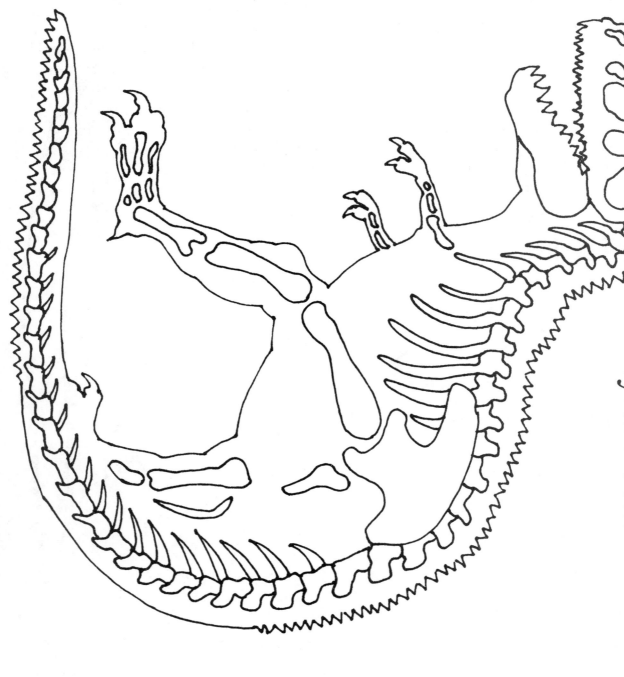

Parasaurolophus

Parasaurolophus (pair-a-sawr-o-low-fuss) "Like a Crested Lizard,"
Cretaceous Period

These large, vegetarian dinosaurs lived in scrubland and forested areas. They probably travelled in large herds. A strange-looking tube attached to the back of the head of Parasaurolophus was hollow and connected the nose and throat. Scientists now think this tube was used as a sound amplifier, and that Parasaurolophus and other similar dinosaurs could make loud trumpeting noises much like elephants do today. These noises would have helped the animals keep in communication as the herd moved from place to place. Parasaurolophus grew to lengths of over 9 meters (30 feet), weighed more than 4,500 kilograms (5 tons), and lived in the southwestern United States and western Canada.

Parasaurolophus

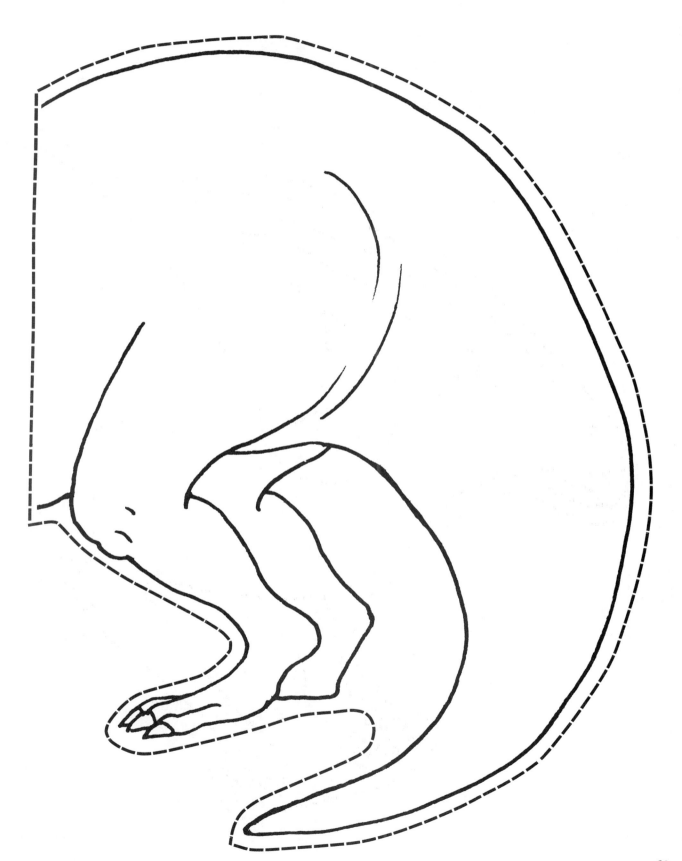

Triceratops

Triceratops (try-sayr-a-tops) "Three-Horned Eye,"
Cretaceous Period

Triceratops, and other similar dinosaurs, were the rhinoceroses of the Cretaceous period. They travelled in large herds, much as bison do, feeding on grass and small plants. Triceratops was one of the most common dinosaurs in North America, and also one of the last to become extinct. Like a rhinoceros, Triceratops was bulky and armed with large defensive spikes on its face. These spikes were used for protection against large meat-eaters like Tyrannosaurus and Albertosaurus. Males were much bigger than females. A large male could grow to more than 9 meters (30 feet) and weigh more than 10,000 kilograms (12 tons). Triceratops' skeletons are found in Wyoming, Montana, and the Dakotas in the United States and in western Canada.

Triceratops

Name _____

Date _____

Ultrasaurus

Ultrasaurus (ul-tra-sawr-us) "Greatest Lizard," Cretaceous Period

Ultrasaurus is still only a scientific nickname, as the species has not yet been officially named. This long-necked dinosaur is only known from a few bones, but these show that this animal was probably the longest, and maybe the largest, land animal that ever lived. The dinosaur was over 30 meters (100 feet) tall. The neck of Ultrasaurus, alone, was more than 24 meters (80 feet) long. The animal probably fed on giant conifer trees that were over 30 meters (100 feet) tall. Ultrasaurus, then, was probably the "super giraffe" of the Cretaceous dinosaurs. The bones of Ultrasaurus have only been found in southwestern Colorado. At the end of the Cretaceous period, this area was covered with forests of giant trees larger than redwoods or sequoias.

Ultrasaurus

© 1989

Name _____

Date _____

PLANT EATERS

(Herbivores)

▮ Mouths small in proportion to head.

▮ Many large molars and nipping incisor teeth; some have beaks.

▮ Often quadripedal (walked on all four legs). Examples are Hadrosaurus ("duck-billed"); Iguanodontids, and Pachycephalosaurs ("bone-headed"). Some were partly quadripedal; they used all four legs when feeding and caring for their young, but usually walked upright on their stronger hind legs.

▮ Forearms longer than carnivores, with grasping fingers (Iguanodon) for grabbing vegetation.

▮ Some herbivores laid eggs.

▮ Because of the lack of fossil eggs, it is believed that some herbivores gave birth to live young.

▮ Probably drank water like today's birds (getting a mouthful of water and tipping the head straight back).

▮ Strictly plant eaters (mostly conifers, palms, ferns).

Minmi

Minmi (min-me)
Late Cretaceous Period

Minmi was a small, armored ankylosaur, probably 3 meters (10 feet) long or less. Minmi was named for a geological deposit (the Minmi Member of the Bungil Formation) north of Roma, southern Queensland, Australia. Minmi has the shortest generic name of any dinosaur to date.

Minmi

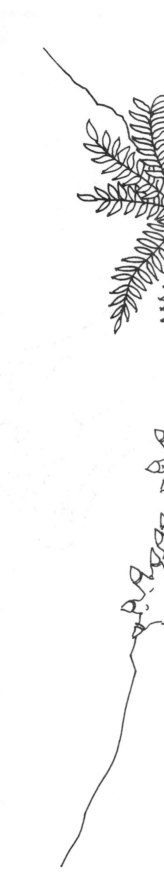

Worksheet A (front)
Stuffed Minmi

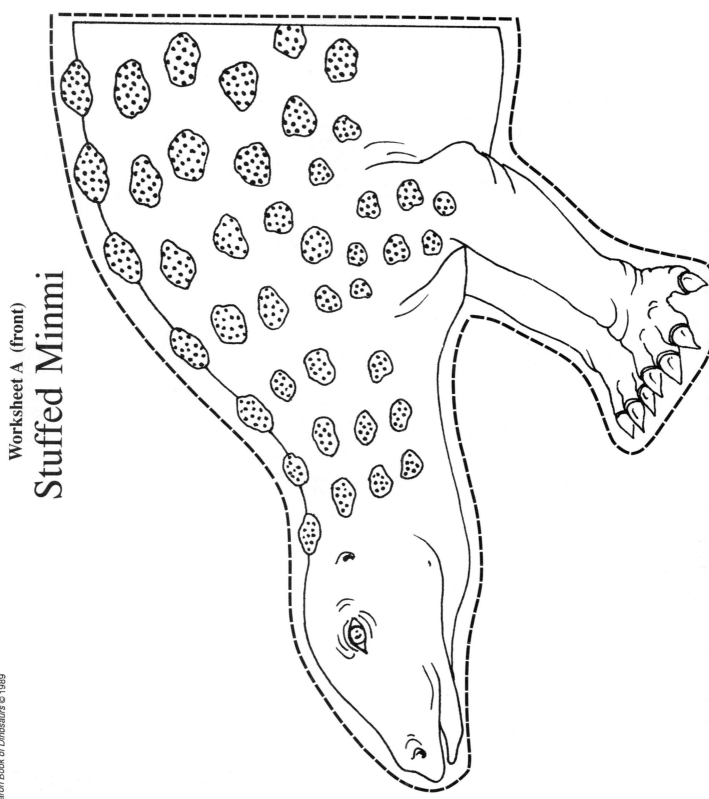

Worksheet A (back)
Stuffed Minmi

The Big Fearon Book of Dinosaurs © 1989

Worksheet B (front)

Stuffed Minmi

Stuffed Minmi

The Big Fearon Book of Dinosaurs © 1989

Hidden Dinosaur

Minmi

Name _____

Date _____

Dacentrurus

Dacentrurus (dah-cen-true-roos) "Pointed Tail,"
Late Jurassic Period

Remains of this dinosaur have been found in Wiltshire, England; France; and Portugal. In Portugal, eggs were found that possibly belonged to Dacentrurus. This animal was about 4.5 meters (15 feet) long and had erect, paired spikes which ran along its neck, back, and tail.

Toothpick Spikes
Dacentrurus

77 Name _____

Date _____

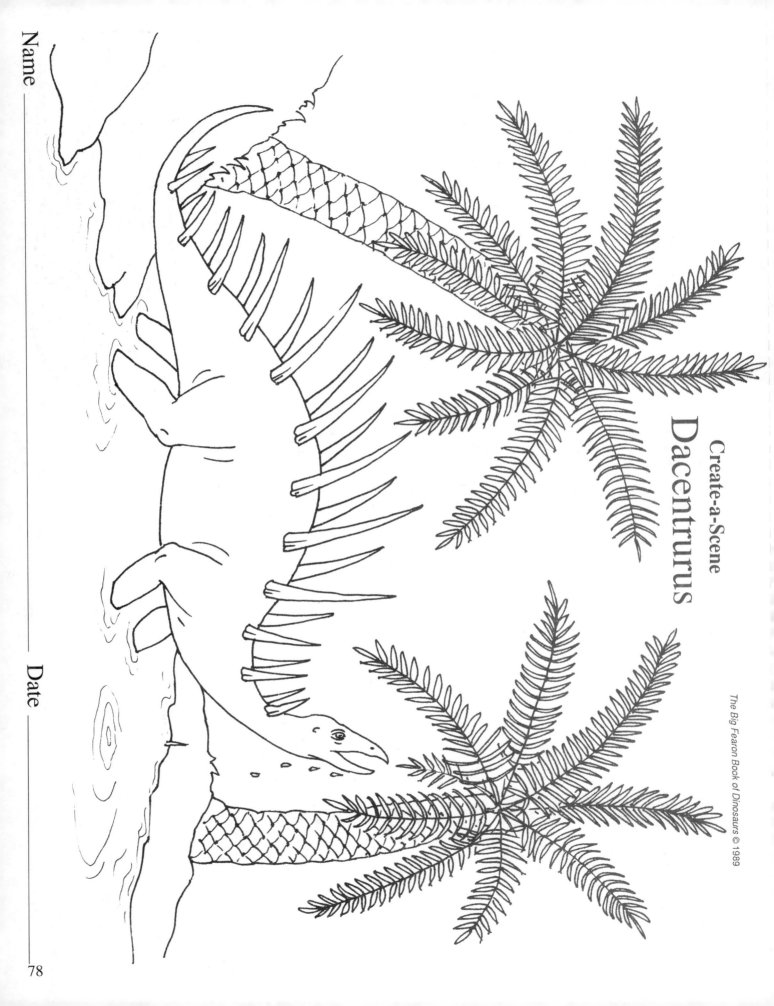

Create-a-Scene

Dacentrurus

The Big Fearon Book of Dinosaurs © 1989

Defensive Movement
Dacentrurus

Meat-Eater
(Megalosaurus)

Plant-Eater
(Dacentrurus)

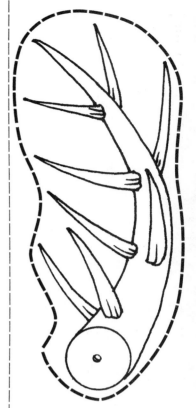

Name _____

Date _____

Tsintaosaurus

Tsintaosaurus (sin tao-sawr-us) "Lizard from Tsintao," Late Cretaceous Period

This hadrosaur is from Shandong, China. It had a solid crest which was shaped like a vertical blade above the eyes. The crest was formed by extended nasal bones. This duck-billed dinosaur probably grew to about 6 meters (20 feet).

Sequencing

1

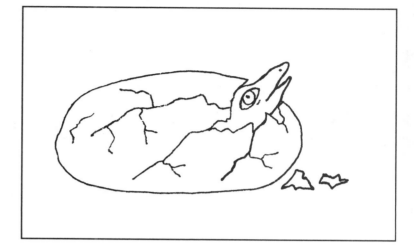

2

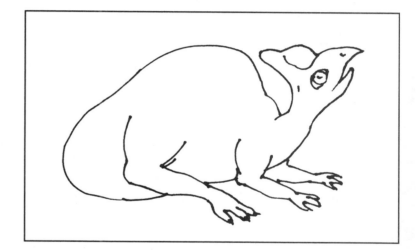

3

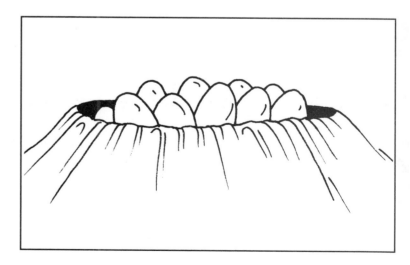

Name _____ Date _____

Tsintaosaurus

Tsintaosaurus

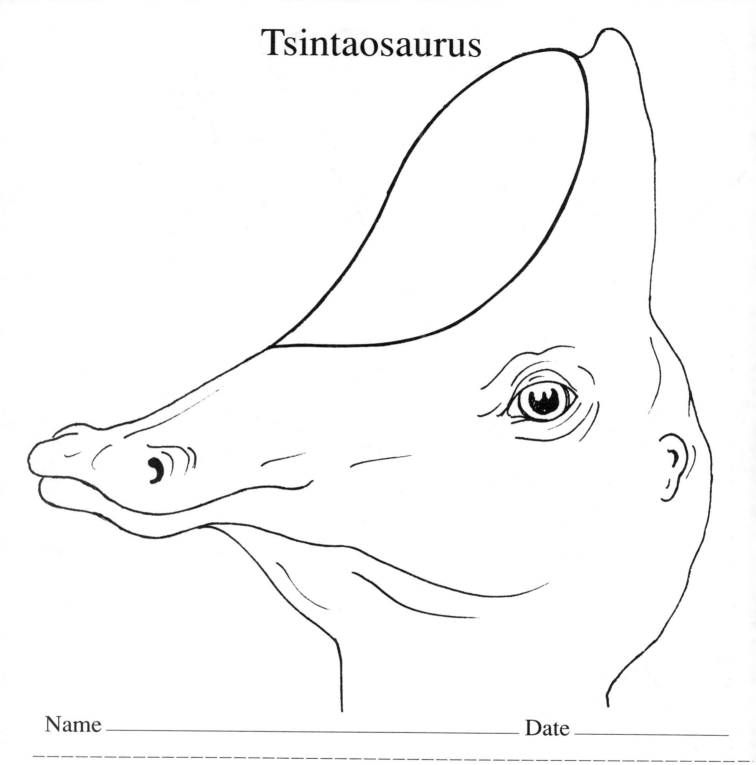

Name _____ Date _____

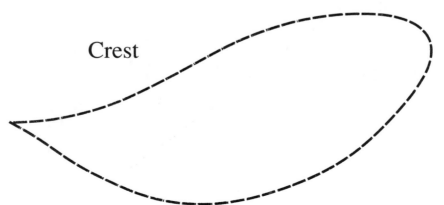

Crest

Rebbachisaurus

Rebbachisaurus (re-back-i-sawr-us) "Rebbachi Lizard,"
Late Cretaceous Period

This sauropod is known from Morocco and Tunisia. It probably reached a length of about 18 meters (60 feet). The elongated dorsal vertebrae produced a characteristic "fin" down its back. This dinosaur could reach tall vegetation with its long neck.

The Big Fearon Book of Dinosaurs © 1989

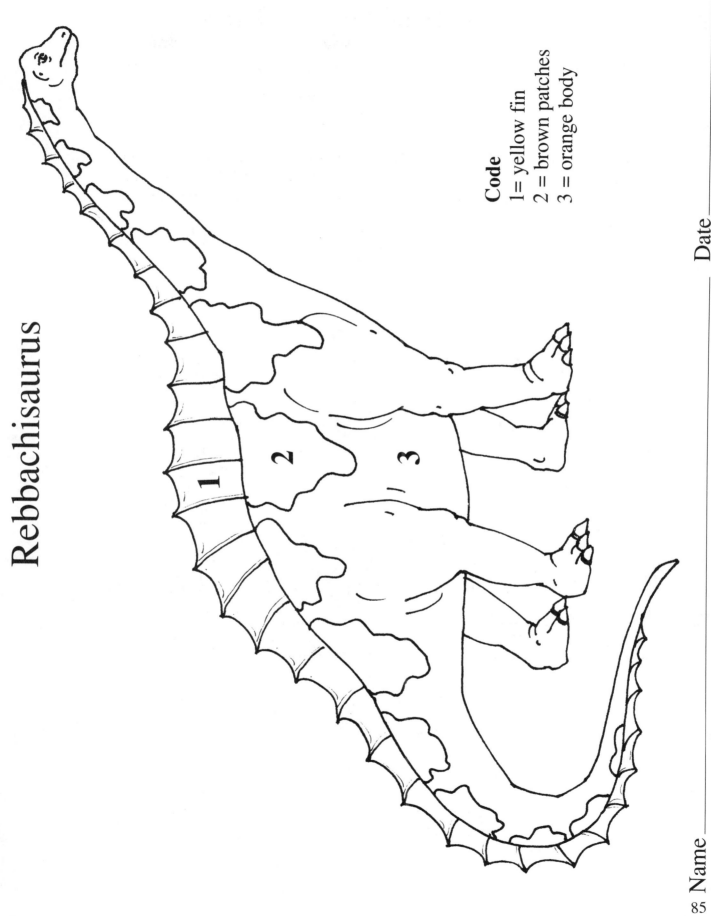

Rebbachisaurus

Code
1 = yellow fin
2 = brown patches
3 = orange body

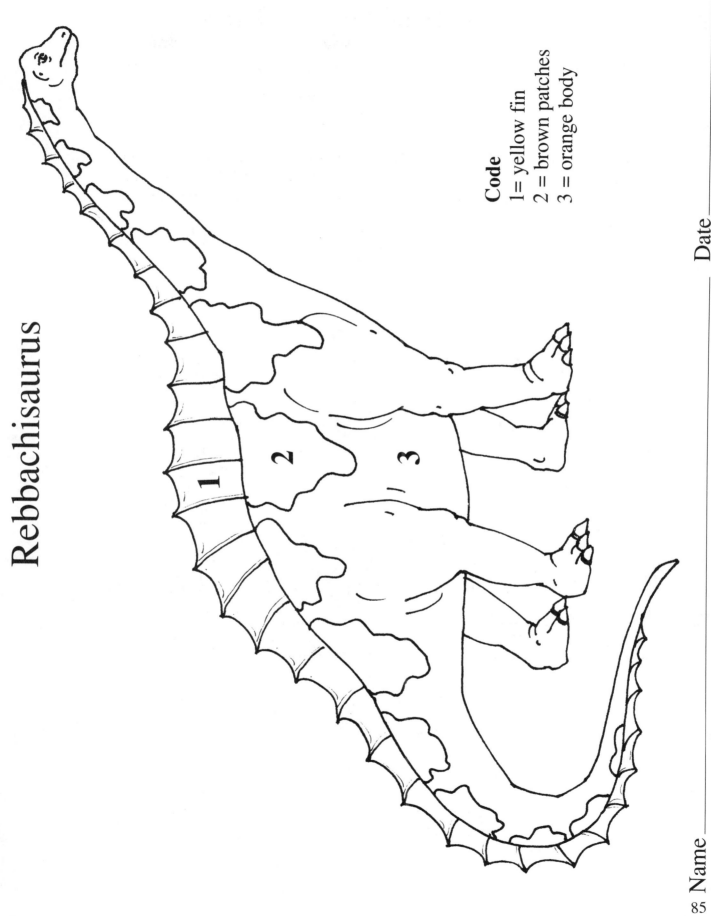

The Big Fearon Book of Dinosaurs © 1989

Name

Date

Rebbachisaurus

Rebbachisaurus
Dino-Diet

Name _____

Date _____

Rebbachisaurus

Dino-diet

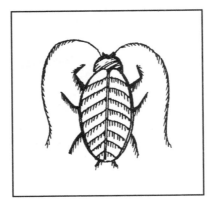

The Big Fearon Book of Dinosaurs © 1989

Pachyrhinosaurus

Pachyrhinosaurus (pack-e-rhino-sawr-us) "Thick-nosed Lizard,"
Late Cretaceous Period

This unusual looking ceratopsian is from the St. Mary River and Horseshoe Canyon deposits of Alberta, Canada. This dinosaur is closely related to Styracosaurus. The frill may have had short spikes, and the upper part of the skull had a coarse knob covering the snout between the eyes. There were two large spikes at the top of the frill, and two stubby knobs near the nostrils. As with other ceratopsians, Pachyrhinosaurus had a beak that was used for chopping vegetation and molars that were used for chewing. Pachyrhinosauras measured about 6 meters (18 feet) in length.

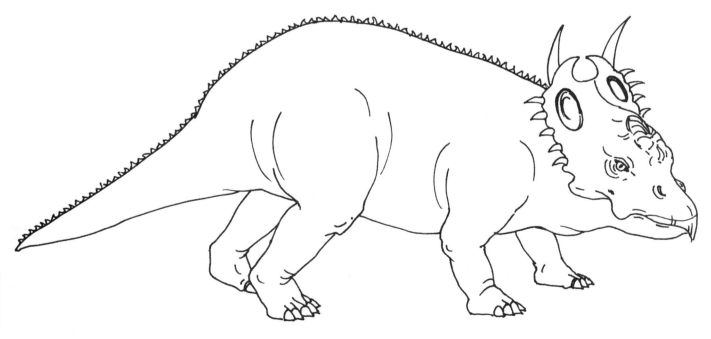

Pachyrhinosaurus

Design-a-Dino

Dinosaur Match

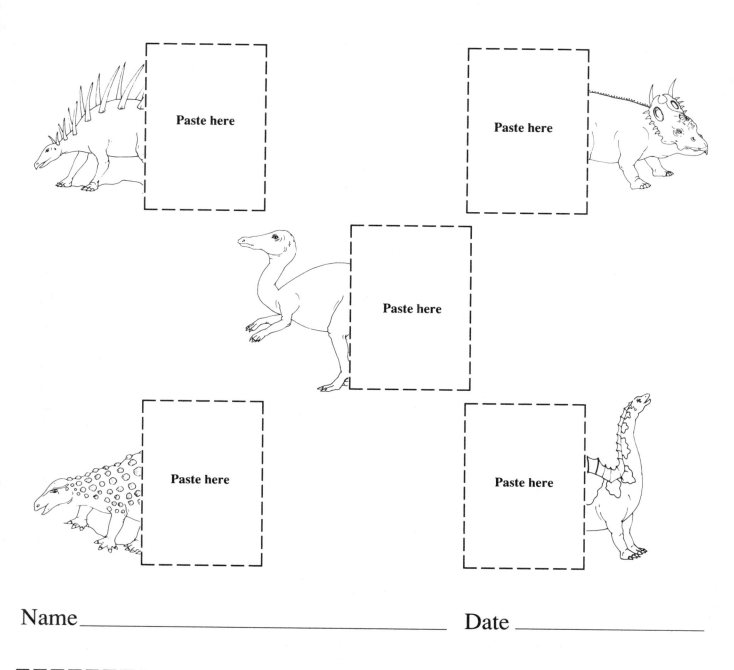

Paste here

Paste here

Paste here

Paste here

Paste here

Name_____ Date_____

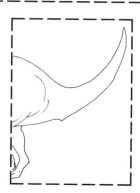 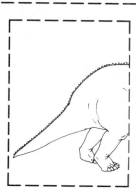 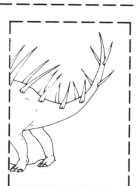 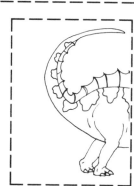

Claosaurus

Claosaurus (clow-sawr-us) "Branched Lizard"
Late Cretaceous Period

This hadrosaur is from North America. It is both the oldest and the most primitive from this area. This genus is somewhat smaller, 3.6 meters (12 feet) long, than the later noncrested hadrosaurs. Its teeth were primitive and its tail perhaps longer than those of its descendants.

The Big Fearon Book of Dinosaurs © 1989

Claosaurus

Measuring Scale

1 ⊂⊃ = .3 meter (1 foot)

I am _____ meters or _____ feet long.

Name _____

Date _____

Matching Babies to Adults

Matching Parts

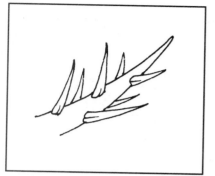 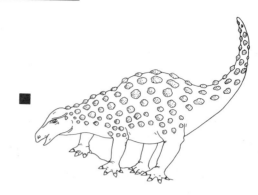

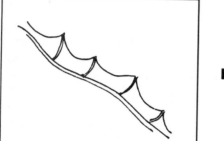 

 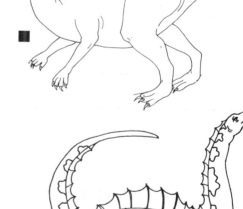

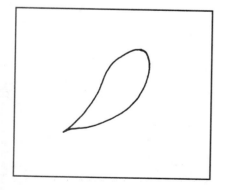

Name _____ Date _____

MEAT EATERS

(Carnivores)

▌ Large mouths in proportion to head.

▌ Overly large teeth in proportion to mouth.

▌ Streamlined bodies and well-developed hind legs (for running after prey).

▌ All bipedal (walked on two hind legs).

▌ Forearms usually small; armed with very large, cat-like claws.

▌ Because of the lack of fossil eggs, it is believed that most carnivores gave birth to live young.

▌ Large rigid tail used for balance (like a kangaroo tail).

▌ Ate only meat.

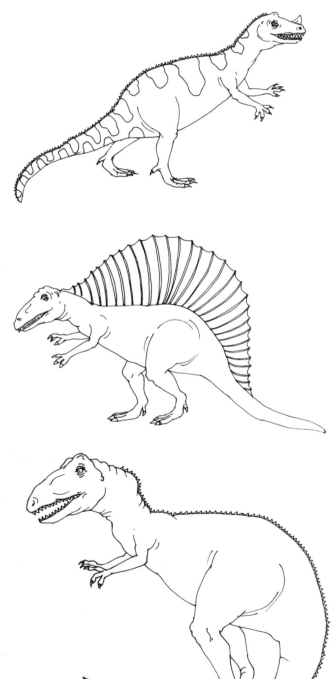

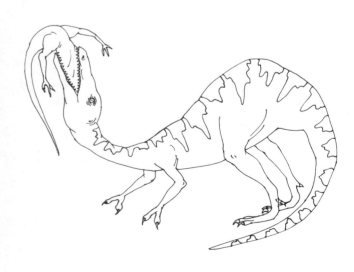

Kakuru

Kakuru (ka-koo-roo), "Rainbow Lizard,"
Early Cretaceous Period

The genus is based on a tibia found in Southern Australia. During the Cretaceous Period, Australia's southern end was very close to Antarctica. The weather was very cold, with heavy snowfall in winter. Kakuru probably had feathers for warmth. It was a relatively small dinosaur of approximately 3 meters (10 feet) in length.

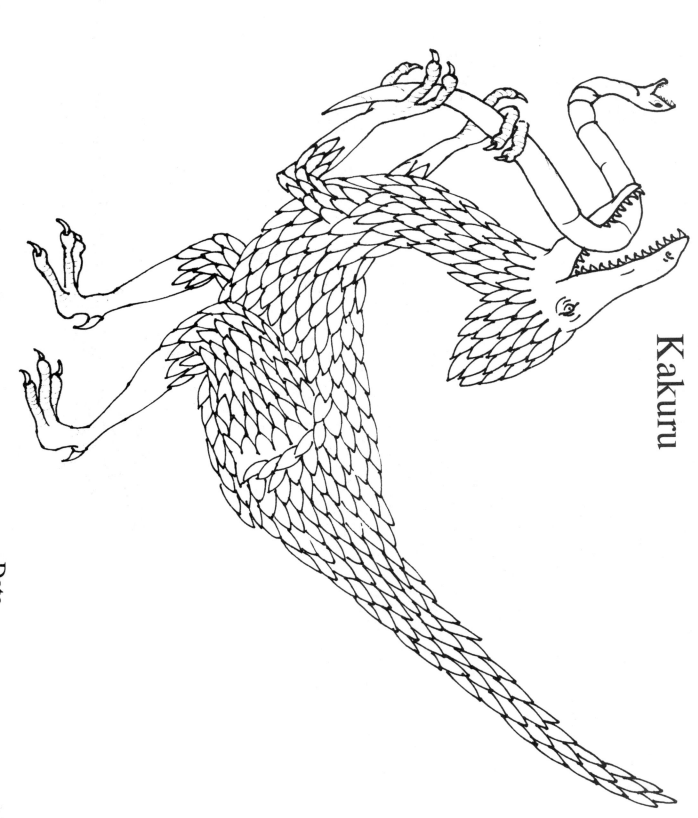

Kakuru

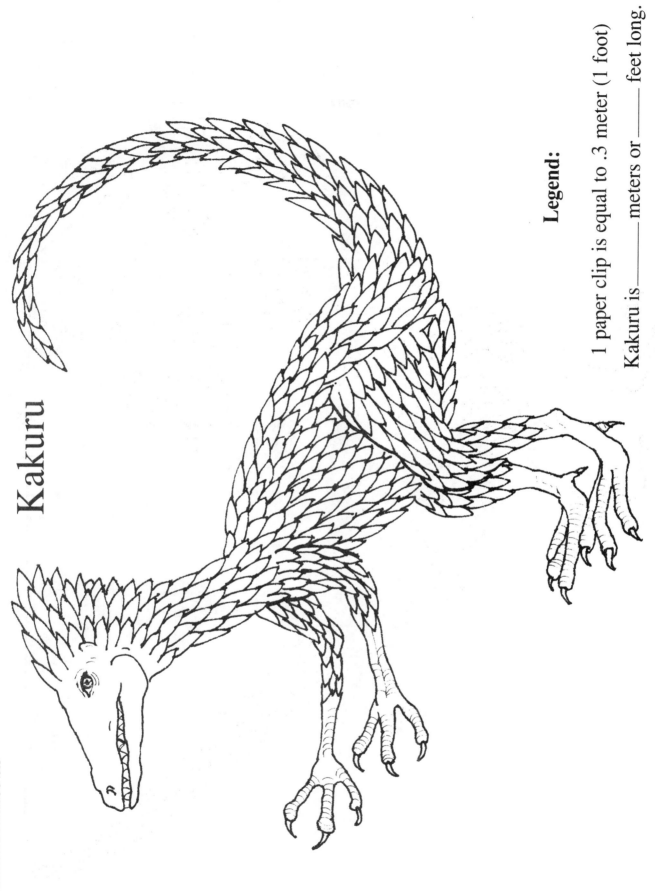

Kakuru

Legend:

1 paper clip is equal to .3 meter (1 foot)

Kakuru is _____ meters or _____ feet long.

Name _____

Date _____

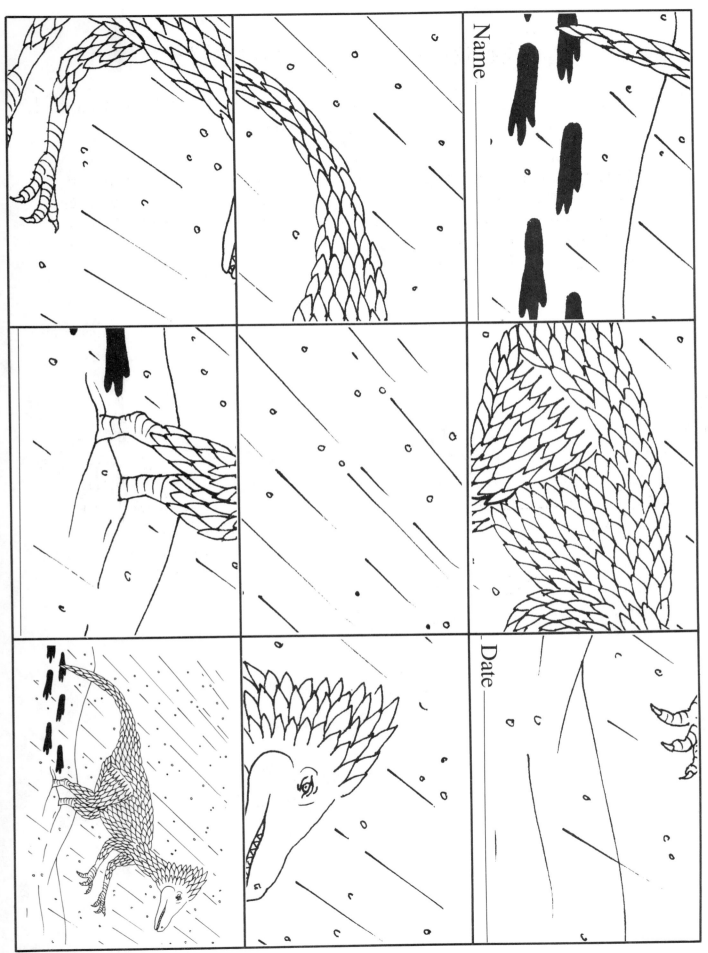

The Big Fearon Book of Dinosaurs © 1989

Stenonychosaurus

Stenonychosaurus (sten-o-nike-o-sawr-us) "Narrow-Clawed Lizard,"
Late Cretaceous Period

Stenonychosaurus was a lightly built dinosaur of around 2 meters (6.5 feet) in length. It had slender arms with thin fingers. It had long, slim back legs, and a long, pointed tail. Stenonychosaurus was a very fast-moving flesh-eater with large eyes that enabled it to see well at night. The brain of this dinosaur was large. Its reflexes were quick and its senses well-developed.

Stenonychosaurus

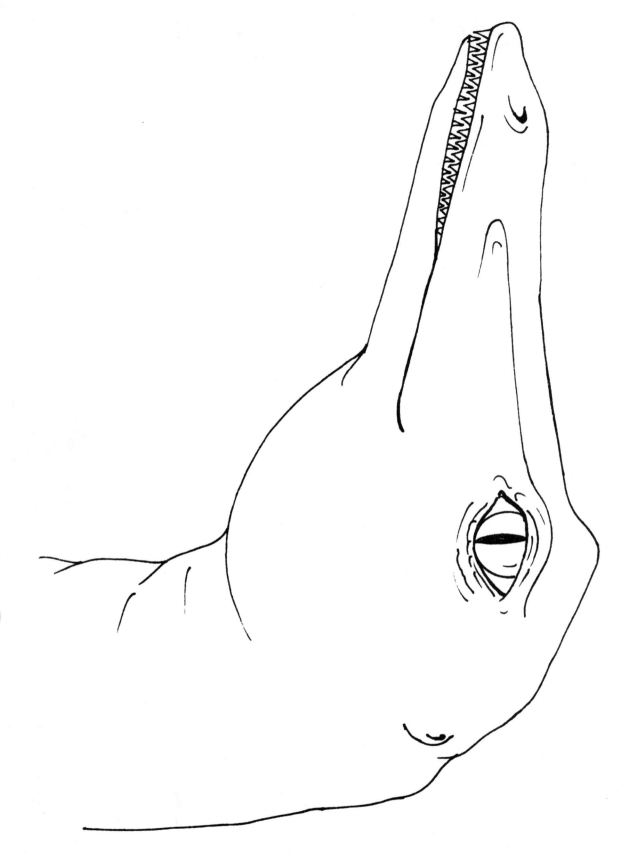

Stenonychosaurus Diet

Name_____ Date_____

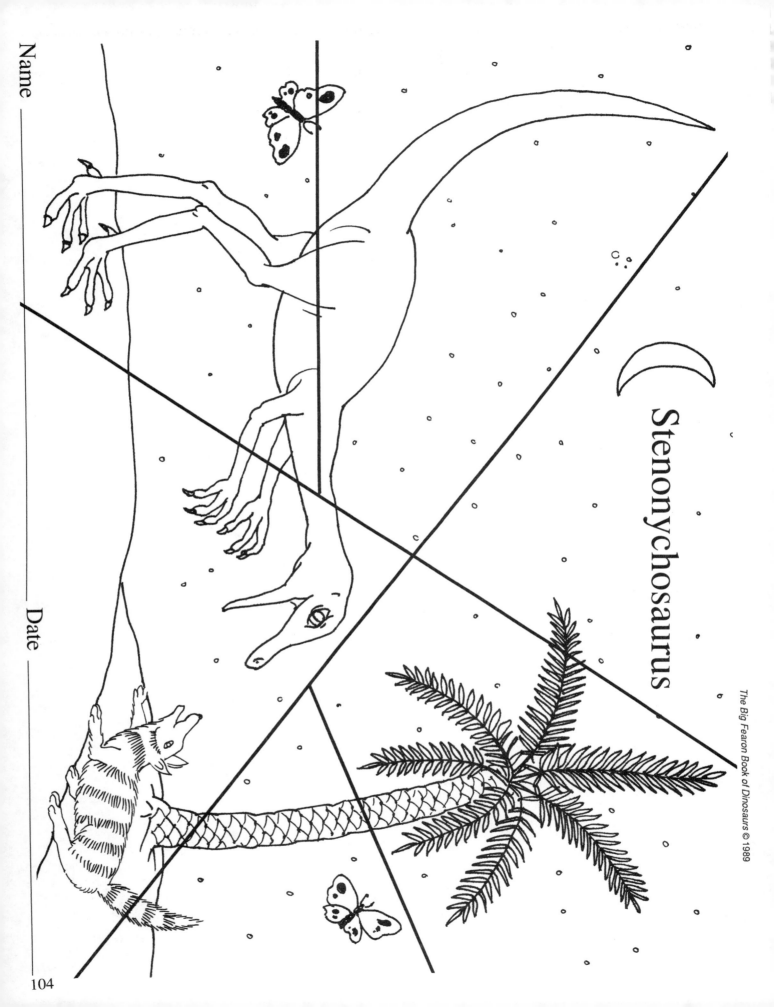

Name

Date

Stenonychosaurus

104

Spinosaurus

Spinosaurus (spine-oh-sawr-us) "Spiny Lizard," Early Cretaceous Period

Spinosaurus was a meat-eating dinosaur that had a sail of skin on its back. The sail was held up by tall spines on the backbone. The sail was used to control body heat, keeping Spinosaurus warm in winter and cool in summer. The Spinosaurus was a great dinosaur that grew to lengths of 12 meters (40 feet). Skeletal remains have been found in Nigeria and Egypt.

Spinosaurus

Spinosaurus

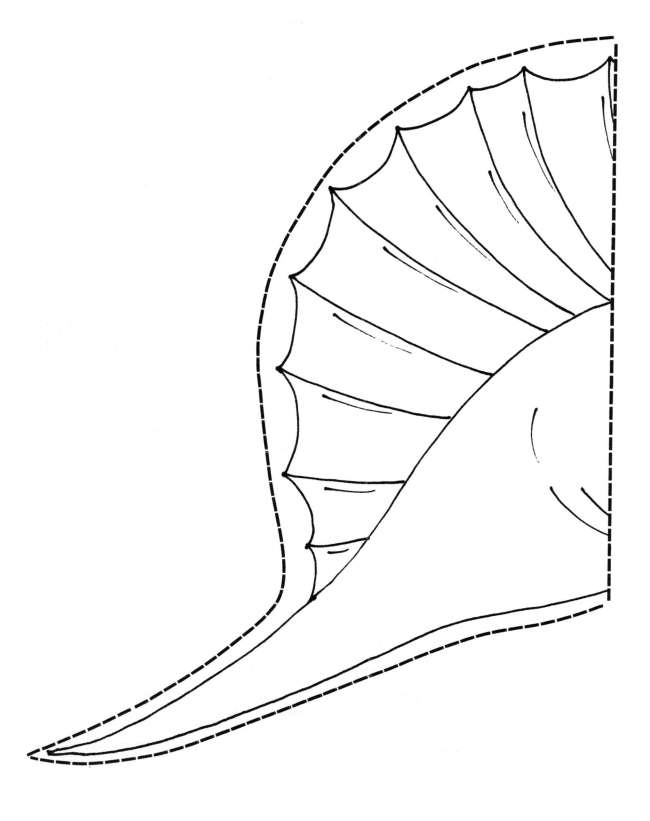

Spinosaurus

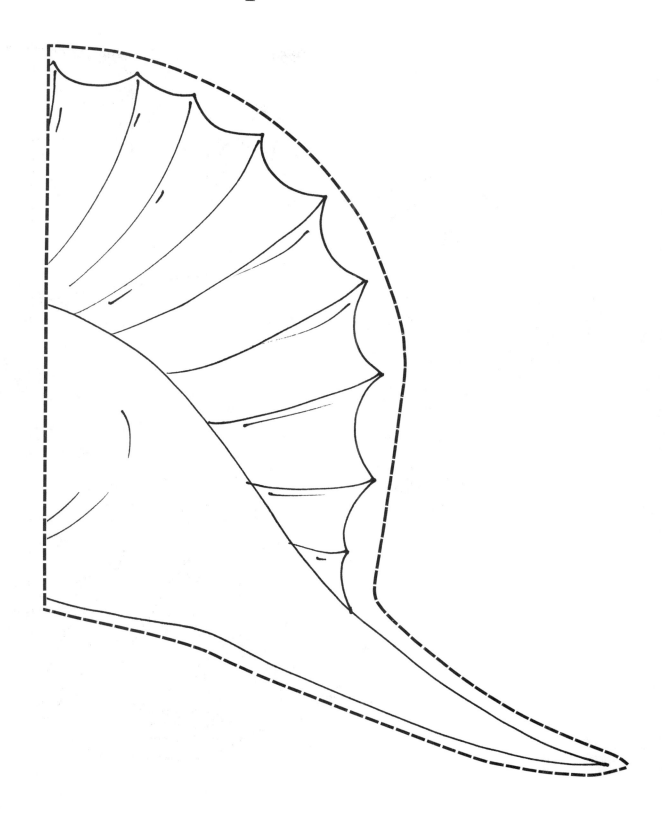

Spinosaurus

Spinosaurus

Name _____

Date _____

Ceratosaurus

Ceratosaurus (sai-rat-o-sawr-us) "Horned Lizard,"
Late Jurassic Period

The Ceratosaurus lived in of North America. It grew to lengths of 4.6-6 meters (15-20 feet) and looked similar to the Allosaurus. This dinosaur is the only known meat-eater to have had one horn. It had a huge head and saber-like teeth. There were bony knobs above each eye. The Ceratosaurus walked on two legs. Its front legs were short and had four fingers. Its two back legs had three-toed, birdlike feet.

Ceratosaurus

Teeth for Ceratosaurus

Ceratosaurus

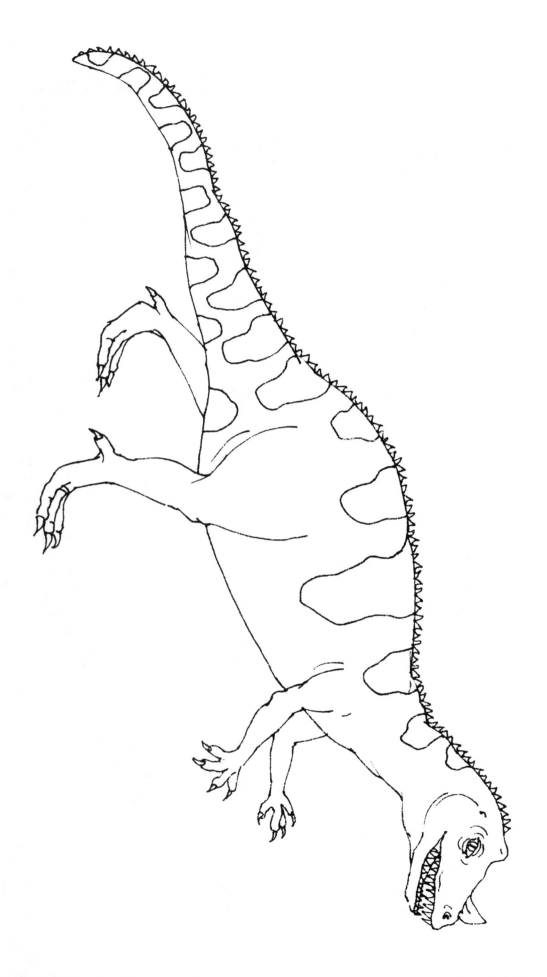

The Big Fearon Book of Dinosaurs © 1989

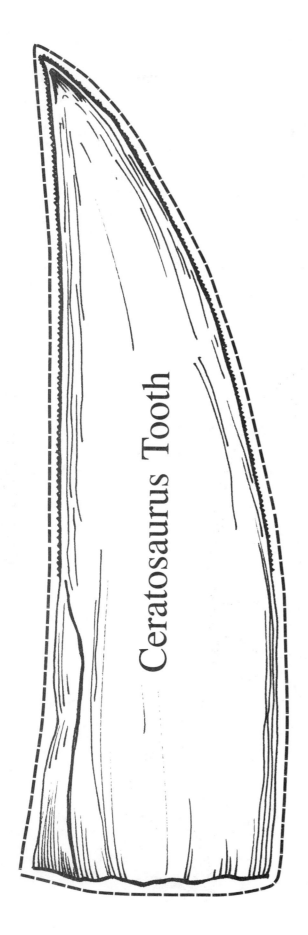

Ceratosaurus Tooth

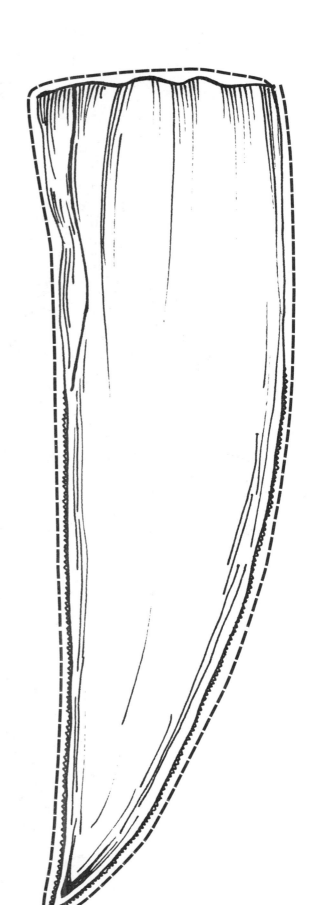

Name

Date

Allosaurus

Allosaurus (al-o-sawr-us) "Different Lizard,"
Late Jurassic Period

Allosaurus lived in the late Jurassic Period. It was one of the main meat-eating dinosaurs of North America. The Allosaurus fed on many well-known dinosaurs such as the Stegosaurus and Apatosaurus. Allosaurus grew to lengths of 10.6 meters (35 feet). It had sharp teeth and sharp claws. When walking upright, it used its tail for balance. Allosaurus had a ridge of bone that ran along the top of its skull from between the eyes to the tip of the snout.

116

Allosaurus

Name

Date

Worksheet B

Allosaurus Skeleton

The Big Fearon Book of Dinosaurs © 1989

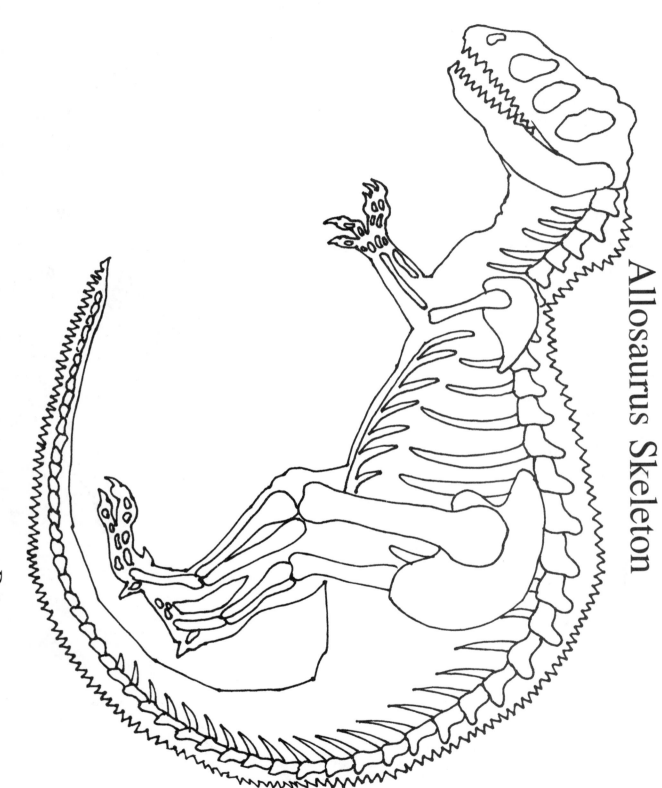

Allosaurus Bag Puppet–Head

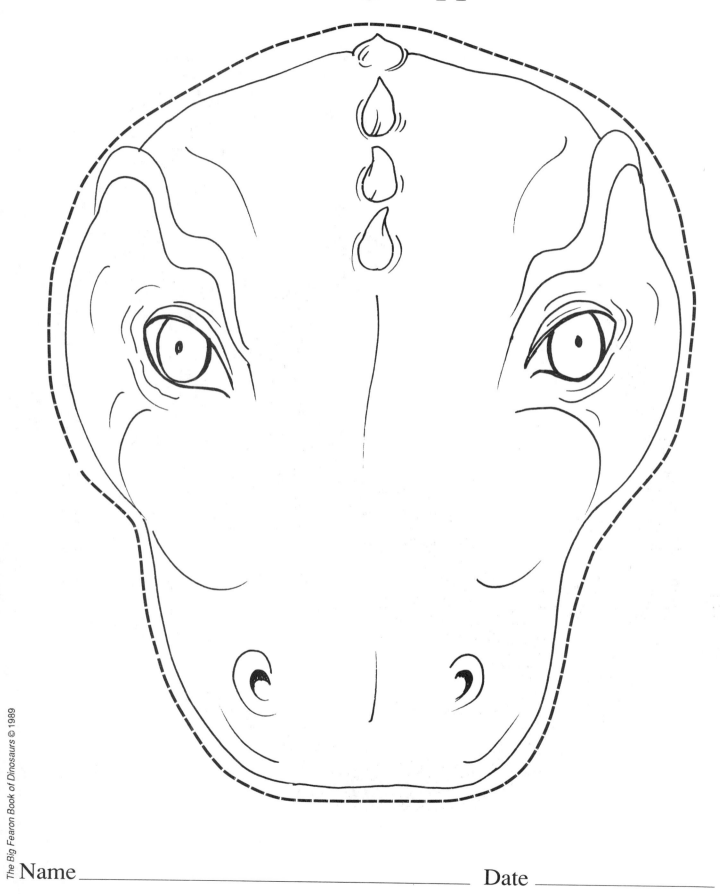

Name_____ Date _____

Allosaurus Bag Puppet–Tail

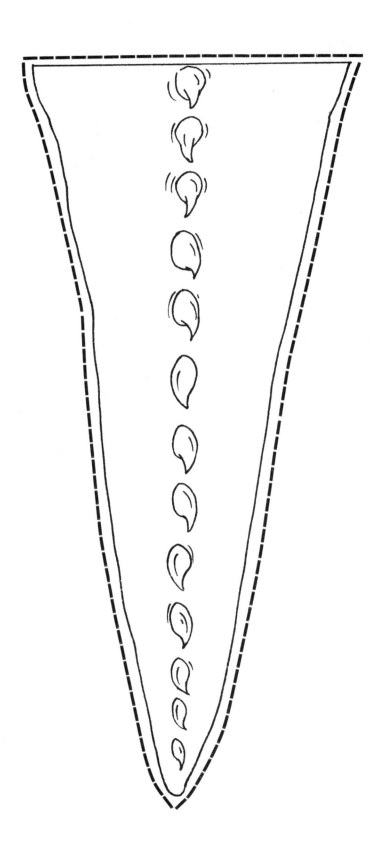

Allosaurus Bag Puppet–Body

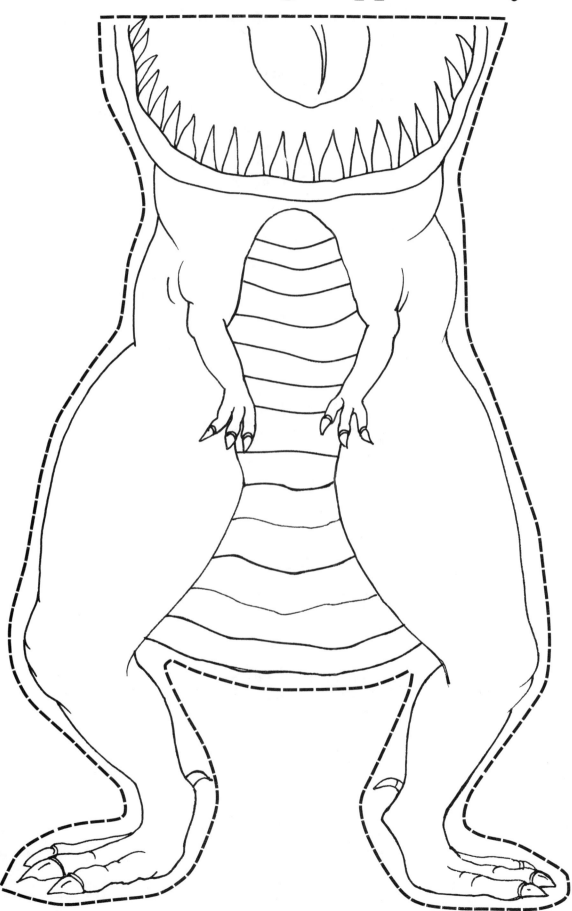

Name _____

Date _____

Hunting Scene Puzzle

Compsognathus

Compsognathus (komp-sow-nay-thus) "Elegant Jaw,"
Late Jurassic Period

Found in Southern Germany and France, the Compsognathus is one of the smallest known dinosaurs. The animals grew to a length of 60-90 centimeters (2-3 feet). About the size of a large rooster. Compsognathus was a flesh-eating dinosaur that walked upright. A complete skeleton of Compsognathus was found in Germany in 1861.

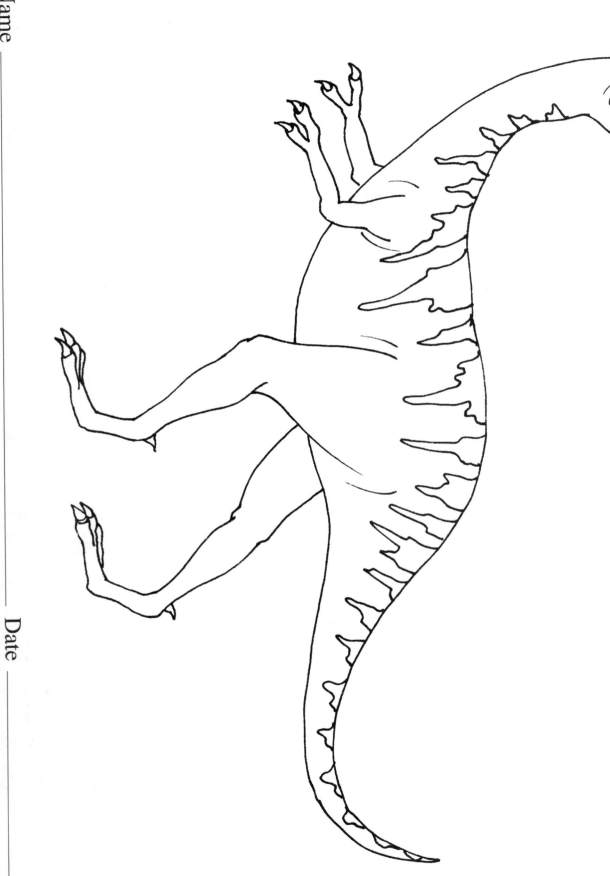

Compsognathus

Worksheet A

Compsognathus Diet

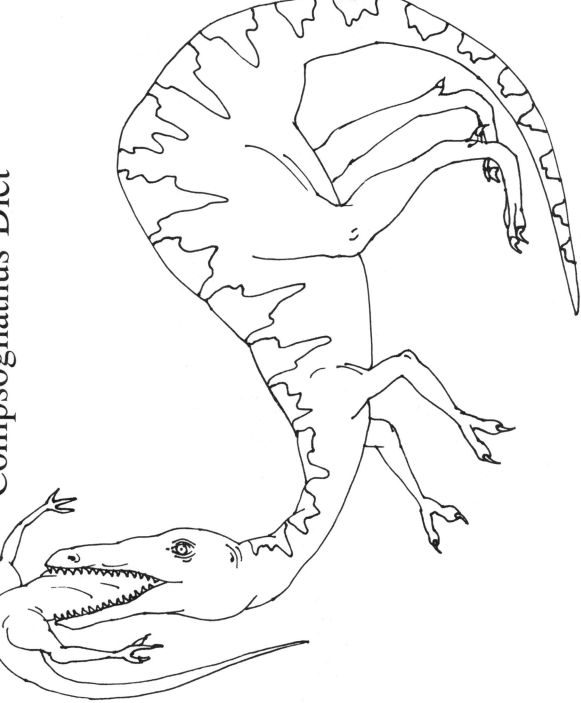

Name _____

Date _____

Compsognathus Diet

Match the Parts to the Dinosaurs

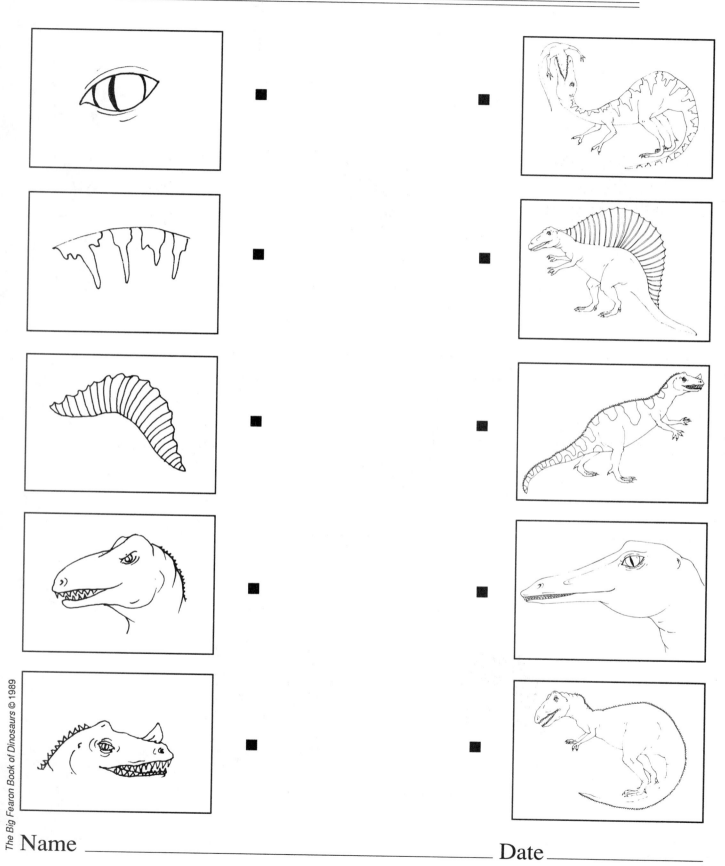

Name _____

Date _____

Dino-Tale Creative Writing

Name _____ Date _____